PricewaterhouseCoopers
Guide to Tax and
Financial Planning, 2006

PRICEWATERHOUSECOOPERS

Guide to Tax and Financial Planning, 2006

How the 2005 Tax Law Changes Affect You

PricewaterhouseCoopers LLP

WILEY

John Wiley & Sons, Inc.

NOTE: This Guide was prepared and published based on the tax rules and regulations in effect as of November 7, 2005.

Published by John Wiley & Sons, Inc., Hoboken, New Jersey.

Published simultaneously in Canada.

For general information on our other products and services or for technical support, please contact our Customer Care Department within the United States at (800) 762-2974, outside the United States at (317) 572-3993 or fax (317) 572-4002.

Wiley also publishes its books in a variety of electronic formats. Some content that appears in print may not be available in electronic books. For more information about Wiley products, visit our web site at www.wiley.com.

Library of Congress Cataloging-in-Publication Data:

ISBN-13 978-0-471-74557-0
ISBN-10 0-471-74557-X

Printed in the United States of America.
10 9 8 7 6 5 4 3 2 1

ACKNOWLEDGMENTS

A publication of this kind does not come together without the invaluable contributions of many. In particular, we would like to thank John Cooper, Jeffrey Davis, Christine Lamprecht, Tina Malek, William Pietrangelo, Paul Schlather, Amanda Stackpoole, Kelly Traw, and Rich Wagman for their important contributions.

This book is dedicated to the many partners and professionals of PricewaterhouseCoopers LLP, who have spent a significant portion of their careers working with clients in developing strategies designed to help build, preserve, and maximize wealth.

Michael B. Kennedy
Partner, Private Company Services
Personal Financial Services Practice

Bernard S. Kent
Partner, Private Company Services
Personal Financial Services Practice

Karl T. Weger
Partner, Private Company Services
Personal Financial Services Practice

CONTENTS

INTRODUCTION

To life's two proverbial certainties—death and taxes—we can safely add a third related one: tax *changes*. Year-in and year-out, the Internal Revenue Code presents a moving target. Congress, while keeping up a steady stream of complaints about the Tax Code's complexity and impenetrability, just can't seem to leave it alone. Whether there is a major overhaul or some relatively minor tinkering, there is always something new to worry about or profit from. Sometimes fairness or simplification is the goal; other times it's a break just for a small group of taxpayers; occasionally it's across-the-board relief.

In the past several years, Congress has made a great number of changes that phase-in over several years, take effect at different times, or expire at set dates. Layered on this complexity are more than two dozen rules that are adjusted annually for inflation. These varying dates and inflation adjustments make using the new rules and planning for tomorrow extremely confusing and complex. And, as we go to press, Congress is poised to make additional changes that you want to watch out for.

How can you keep up with all the changes and know which of them can help you save money and plan for your future? This book gives you the tools you need to begin to sort things out and put them straight. It identifies the major areas of the tax law that have been, or will be, changed, including individual income tax rate reductions, reduced capital gains, and dividends tax rates. It also shows how to use liberalized tax breaks to pay for education costs and how to maximize the expanded tax breaks for company-sponsored retirement plans and IRAs.

This book spells out the most important features of all these changes as well as the impact of important business tax breaks. It clearly explains the opportunities for new tax-saving advantages and strategies now, and in the coming years.

About PricewaterhouseCoopers

PricewaterhouseCoopers (www.pwc.com) provides industry-focused assurance, tax, and advisory services for public and private clients. More than 120,000 people in 144 countries connect their thinking, experience, and solutions to build public trust and enhance value for clients and their stakeholders.

PricewaterhouseCoopers' Private Company Services practice is an integrated team of audit, tax, personal finance and advisory professionals who focus on the unique needs of private companies and their owners. Within the practice, dedicated professionals concentrate on the needs of manufacturing, retail, wholesale and distribution, construction, food and beverage, and private equity portfolio companies, as well as on the needs of law firms and other service organizations. Our Private Company Services professionals are committed to delivering cost-effective, practical solutions and responsive services with the quality clients expect from PricewaterhouseCoopers.

PricewaterhouseCoopers' personal financial planning professionals help clients design strategies that can effectively preserve, enhance

and transfer their wealth effectively. Over 350 dedicated professionals provide comprehensive financial planning services, including
estate and gift tax planning, income tax advisory and preparation,
compensation and stock option planning, investment advice, retirement planning, and charitable giving strategies.

For more information about PricewaterhouseCoopers' Private Company Services practice, visit www.pwc.com/pcs.

How to Use This Book

Chapter by chapter, we clarify the vital sections of new tax rules,
with concrete examples that tell taxpayers what they need to know
to build a solid base for planning and to begin mapping their own
dollar-saving strategies. However, oversimplification is dangerous.
We strongly recommend that taxpayers understand at least the basic
provisions of the law before planning—that is why we wrote this
book. Here's what lies ahead:

- Chapter 1 spells out the key elements of the most recent tax law
  changes at work today, explaining briefly what each major provision and change does, how it works, and its timing.

- The laws' impact on investments and stock options is the subject
  of Chapter 2. There are major changes that will affect most investment plans.

- Retirement planning should be part of each taxpayer's strategy
  from the beginning of employment. Chapter 3 discusses how to
  make planning for retirement a reality, and what changes in planning the new laws will entail.

- The tax advantages of home ownership have been accepted wis-
  dom for decades. But Chapter 4 explores the subtle differences
  the new laws will make when it comes to owning a home.

- The escalating costs of higher education can make paying tuition
  and other expenses difficult. Fortunately, the tax law provides incentives for both saving for education in the future as well as

paying for education now. Chapter 5 covers how to maximize tax law opportunities to save and pay for education.

- Paying for medical expenses has become more challenging as health-care costs continue to rise. Tax law changes, explained in Chapter 6, provide some important options for paying health-care costs on a tax-advantaged basis.

- How can you structure your estate for a time when the "death tax" is gradually phasing out, only to reappear after 2010? Chapter 7 offers estate planning ideas.

- Chapter 8 gives detailed guidance on the rules for deducting charitable contributions.

- Chapter 9 sums up important strategies for year-end tax planning in a quick planning guide.

- When preparing your taxes, moving deductions to the previous tax year can save significant dollars. Chapter 10 describes those deductions that may be best to accelerate.

- Chapter 11 applies the same year-end tax-saving principles to deferring income from one year to the next.

- Chapter 12 describes the alternative minimum tax (AMT), discusses who may be subject to the tax and explains the tax planning implications.

- Year-end planning for business owners incorporates all of the personal strategies previously discussed, but doesn't end there. There are many additional considerations that can generate tax savings for business owners and for their companies that can be found in Chapter 13.

- Chapter 14 explains basic tax concepts as they have evolved in the Tax Code and puts the recent changes into context.

Throughout each chapter are a number of special features. Most of these are *Observations*—brief, clear explanations of specific features of the new law and how they will be applied. There are also occasional passages labeled *Caution,* warning of a possible blunder taxpayers might make based on a misinterpretation of the law. *Leg-*

islative Alerts are highlighted to warn you of possible changes to come. Congress may enact these changes after this book has been completed. In addition, most chapters contain an *Idea Checklist,* offering readers a quick summary of concepts to be used for taking advantage of today's favorable tax rules.

Let's Get Started

It is human, and normal, to be intimidated by the subject of taxes. For most of us, our dealings with the Internal Revenue Service won't end with a royal tap on the shoulder, but we can benefit greatly if we take the initiative and make the effort to overcome such fears. When it comes to taxes, forewarned is forearmed. An investment of time and effort in forming a strategy for the coming years will pay off, year after year.

Tax Law Changes and Financial Planning

Chapter 1

WHAT TAX CHANGES APPLY IN 2005

The old saying that something is "as changeable as the weather" could just as easily be "as changeable as the Tax Code." Rarely does a year go by without some tinkering by Congress. Every couple of decades, there are changes to the Tax Code that require people to fundamentally rethink their tax planning strategies. The old approaches no longer work. Once again, major tax changes in this millennium require that people reconsider their tax situations. Recent reductions in tax rates on ordinary income, capital gains, and dividends have been dramatic. Federal estate taxes are experiencing a period of decline.

The American Jobs Creation Act of 2004 (hereinafter the "2004 Act") made numerous changes that impact individuals. These changes and the planning opportunities they present will be examined in greater detail in this chapter and throughout the book. The major changes impacting individual taxpayers included:

- An election to deduct state and local general sales tax.
- New limits on donations of motor vehicles, boats, and airplanes.
- New donor reporting for noncash charitable contributions.
- A deduction for attorney's fees in discrimination lawsuits.

- Restricting depreciation on sports utility vehicles.
- Expanding the eligible shareholders in S corporations.
- New rules for deferred compensation arrangements.
- Changes to the taxation of personal use of company aircraft and other entertainment expenses.
- New penalties for failing to disclose certain reportable transactions.
- Tougher rules for tax-avoidance expatriation.
- Changes to foreign tax credit carryovers/carrybacks and alternative minimum tax (AMT) limitations.
- Increased penalties for failure to disclose foreign bank accounts.
- Gain recognition on the sale of a principal residence within five years of a like-kind exchange.

Election to Deduct State and Local General Sales Tax

The 2004 Act allows taxpayers who itemize their deductions to deduct state and local sales and use taxes instead of deducting state and local income taxes. States that do not impose an individual income tax generally have higher sales tax rates. Sales taxes were deductible prior to 1987. The 2004 Act attempts to address the disparity in the deductibility of the different methods of state financing.

Individuals who elect to deduct their sales tax have two choices: one alternative is to deduct the actual sales and use tax for the year (maintaining receipts to support the deduction). The other choice is to deduct an amount determined from IRS tables that is based on income, number of dependents, and other factors. The sales tax on motor vehicles and boats can be added to the IRS table amounts.

Taxpayers who pay state income taxes may be better off taking the deduction for sales tax if they have significant purchases subject to sales and use tax. This is particularly true if they are building a house and the sales tax on the cost of materials is stated separately by the contractor. It may also be better to take this deduction in a state with a relatively low income tax rate, and a relatively high sales tax rate.

Taxpayers who pay alternative minimum tax will not receive a federal tax benefit from the sales and use tax deduction. However, taxpayers in certain states can take a deduction for state income tax purposes for the federal sales tax deduction. Thus, taxpayers in these states who are paying federal alternative minimum tax should claim the sales tax deduction on their federal income tax return, even if it is lower than the deduction for state income tax, since states require that the state income tax deduction allowed on the federal return be added back on the state income tax return.

Taxpayers who may benefit from electing the federal sales tax deduction instead of the federal state and local income tax deduction should carefully plan the timing of their large purchases. Also, the decision whether to pay fourth quarter state and local income tax estimated payments in December or January should be made in conjunction with the decision to elect to take the sales tax deduction rather than the state and local income tax deduction. The sales tax deduction election is only effective for tax years beginning after December 31, 2003, and prior to January 1, 2006. For calendar year taxpayers, this means only the 2004 and 2005 tax years.

Donations of Motor Vehicles, Boats, and Airplanes

The 2004 Act limits the deduction available for charitable contributions of used motor vehicles, boats, and airplanes. Charitable deductions are generally limited to the amount the charity receives when it sells the vehicle—unless the charity has made significant use of the vehicle in conducting its activities or made material improvements to the vehicle prior to the sale. A penalty is imposed on charitable organizations that fail to furnish an acknowledgment or knowingly furnish a false acknowledgment (see page 167).

Enhanced Donor Reporting for Noncash Charitable Contributions

The 2004 Act requires increased donor reporting for certain charitable contributions of property other than cash, inventory, or publicly traded securities. Donors, including C corporations, must obtain an appraisal when claiming a deduction exceeding $5,000. If the amount claimed as a deduction exceeds $500,000, the donor must also attach the appraisal to the donor's tax return. All similar items of property donated to one or more organizations will be treated as one property for purposes of determining the applicable thresholds.

Deduction for Attorney's Fees in Discrimination Lawsuits

The 2004 Act clarifies the proper treatment of the deduction for attorney's fees and court costs paid in connection with income from lawsuits involving discrimination or "whistle blowing." The IRS has claimed, with some success, that the attorney's fees are only deductible as a miscellaneous itemized deduction. This usually results in losing some or all of the tax benefit of the deduction, since miscellaneous itemized deductions are not deductible for alternative minimum tax purposes (see page 224).

Under the 2004 Act, attorney's fees in discrimination cases are treated as adjustments to gross income, rather than itemized deductions. As a result, the fees are deductible for alternative minimum tax purposes and have a slightly greater tax benefit for regular tax.

Depreciation on Sports Utility Vehicles

Taxpayers can deduct the full cost of business property under certain conditions (see page 234). The 2004 Act reduced the amount of first-year depreciation that can be claimed on the purchase of a sports utility vehicle that is used in a trade or business. Sports utility vehicles that weigh more than 6,000 pounds are not subject to the restrictive "luxury car" depreciation limits. The ability to write off the full cost of certain sports utility vehicles used for business transportation created a tax incentive to purchase large gas-guzzling vehicles, and this tax incentive was substantially eliminated by the 2004 Act.

Expansion of Eligible Shareholders in an S Corporation

The 2004 Act amends the eligible shareholder rules to qualify to make an S election by allowing a maximum of one hundred shareholders (previously, the limit was seventy-five shareholders). Most significantly, 6 generations of members of the same family can be treated as a single shareholder.

Electing small business trusts (ESBTs) and qualified subchapter S corporation trusts (QSSTs) are included as family members under this election.

Many family businesses that have operated as S corporations have had difficulties maintaining their S corporation status when the ownership of the business was passed down to subsequent generations. This provision essentially guarantees that family succession will not cause disqualification of S corporation status. Also, many more multigenerational family-owned C corporations will be eligible for an S corporation election.

Finally, the 2004 Act allows an electing small business trust to hold S corporation stock regardless of the existence of powers of appointment as long as those powers are not exercised.

Restrictions on Nonqualified Deferred Compensation

The 2004 Act broadly defines the term "nonqualified deferred compensation." It imposes restrictions on the timing and form of deferral elections, the timing of distributions, and the use of certain trusts to fund the arrangements. If these requirements are not met, the participant is subject to current taxation, enhanced underpayment interest, and an additional 20 percent penalty tax. An election to defer compensation must be made no later than the close of the taxable year preceding the year in which the compensation will be earned. In the case of performance-based compensation (based on services performed over a period of at least 12 months) the election may be made up to 6 months prior to the end of the 12-month service period.

Distributions may be made only on separation from service, death, a specified time (or pursuant to a fixed schedule), a change in control of a corporation, an unforeseeable emergency, or the participant's disability. If a plan allows participants to receive a distribution at a specified time or schedule, the participant's initial election must specify the distribution date and must specify the form of payment (e.g., a lump-sum distribution or payments over a 10-year term). Distributions may not be accelerated, with certain limited exceptions, and subsequent elections to further defer an amount are permitted only if the election is made 12 months in advance and the payment is deferred another five years.

These provisions apply to amounts deferred after December 31, 2004, and not to amounts deferred before the effective date or earnings thereon.

Plans that were in effect prior to October 3, 2004, and are not materially modified, may still be operated in accordance with their old terms with respect to amounts deferred before January 1, 2005. For example, if the plan permitted participants to take an early distribution with a penalty (a "haircut" provision), such a distribution may still be made from amounts deferred before January 1, 2005, and earnings thereon.

A material modification to an existing plan after October 3, 2004, such as amending the plan to accelerate vesting, causes the previously deferred amounts and income thereon to become subject to the 2004 Act.

Participants who elect to cancel an outstanding election will be required to include such amounts in income as earned, or if later, when not subject to a substantial risk of forfeiture.

Personal Use of Company Aircraft and Other Entertainment Expenses

Prior law, supported a deduction for the full cost of corporate aircraft even where the employee was a principal owner of the company and used the airplane for personal purposes, as long as the Standard Industry Fare Level (SIFL) safe harbor valuation amount was reported on the employee's W-2 form for personal travel.

The 2004 Act limits a corporation's deduction for the costs associated with a corporate insider's personal use of a corporate aircraft and other entertainment expenses to the amount that is treated as compensation to that individual.

Penalties for Failing to Disclose Certain Reportable Transactions

There are new penalties on individual taxpayers who fail to disclose reportable transactions. For listed transactions, the penalty amount is $100,000, and for other reportable transactions the penalty is $10,000. The penalties apply whenever a taxpayer fails to make a required disclosure, regardless of whether the IRS was aware of (or had audited) the transaction, or whether the taxpayer's position on the merits is sustained. Moreover, no penalty imposed with respect to a listed transaction can be waived under any circumstances. The IRS only has limited authority to rescind penalties with respect to other reportable transactions (and must report any waivers to Congress).

The 2004 Act extends the statute of limitations for any listed transaction that a taxpayer fails to disclose on a timely basis. The 2004 Act extends the statute, solely with respect to the listed transaction, until one year after the date on which the transaction is disclosed to the IRS, either by the taxpayer or by a material advisor. Thus, if the listed transaction is not disclosed, the statute of limitations for that transaction could be open indefinitely.

Tax-Avoidance Expatriation

The 2004 Act strengthens the rules aimed at preventing U.S. citizens and long-term residents from giving up their citizenship or terminating their residency to avoid U.S. taxation. For the 10-year period following the relinquishment of citizenship or the termination of residency, the individual is subject to U.S. taxation on U.S. source income at the tax rates applicable to U.S. citizens, rather than the reduced tax rates that generally apply to nonresident aliens.

Under prior law, there was a subjective determination of whether the individual terminated citizenship or residency with a tax avoidance motive. The 2004 Act changed this to presume a tax avoidance motive if:

1. The individual had average annual net income tax liability in excess of $124,000 (indexed for inflation after 2004) for the five-year period preceding the termination of citizenship or residency.
2. The individual's net worth is $2 million or more.
3. The individual fails to certify compliance with all U.S. tax obligations for the preceding five years.

Foreign Tax Credit Carryover and Carryback

The 2004 Act reduces the number of years that an excess foreign tax credit can be carried back from 2 years to 1 year, and it increases the number of years that an excess foreign tax credit can be carried forward from 5 years to 10 years. The extension of the foreign tax credit carryforward period is effective for foreign tax credits that may be carried to any tax year ending after the date of enactment (October 22, 2004). The reduced carryback period applies to any foreign tax credits arising in tax years beginning after the date of enactment (October 22, 2004).

The 2004 Act also repealed the limitation for AMT purposes that only permitted the AMT foreign tax credit to offset up to 90 percent of the gross AMT. The 90 percent limit is repealed for tax years beginning after December 31, 2004.

Foreign Financial Account Filing

Under prior law, a minimum penalty of $25,000 for failing to report foreign financial accounts only applied to willful violations. The 2004 Act imposes a penalty of up to $10,000 for any failure to file the required report. The 2004 Act also increases the penalty for willful failures to the greater of $100,000 or 50 percent of the transaction or balance in the account at the time of the failure.

Sale of a Principal Residence within Five Years of a Like-Kind Exchange

If an individual acquires a principal residence in a like-kind exchange, the 2004 Act extends the period of time from two years to five years that the residence must be owned before the subsequent sale of the home can qualify for the principal residence gain exclusion. The requirement to live in the home as a principal residence for two of the five years preceding the sale remains unchanged.

Hurricane Katrina Legislation

Tax legislation signed by President Bush on September 23, 2005, provides tax relief for individuals and businesses affected by Hurricane Katrina. This legislation includes a short-term fundraising opportunity for charitable organizations.

The limit on an individual's total deduction for cash charitable contributions—50 percent of the donor's adjusted gross income—has been suspended for gifts paid during the period August 28, 2005, through December 31, 2005. This suspension applies to cash contributions to charitable organizations, but not just those involved with hurricane relief. However the suspension does not apply to contributions to private foundations, supporting organizations, or donor advised funds. Charitable contributions of property, such as stock, are not eligible for the suspension—only charitable contributions of cash qualify.

The new law may create an opportunity for affluent donors who have large balances accumulated in their individual retirement accounts (IRAs) who will not rely on these retirement funds for their personal or family financial needs. In such a case, large cash contributions by a donor age 59½ or older might be funded by taxable or nontaxable distributions from retirement accounts with an offsetting charitable contribution deduction against any taxable distributions.

The portion of the distribution from the donor's IRAs considered taxable will be included in the donor's adjusted gross income (AGI). Since AGI is a factor in determining reductions in a donor's otherwise allowable itemized deductions and personal exemptions, there is likely to be some offset to the full tax benefit of the donor's contribution. However, the contribution will not be subject to the 3 percent reduction discussed on page 14. For some donors seeking a method to contribute substantial funds accumulated in their IRAs and immediately maximize the income tax benefit, the suspension of the 50 percent limit may present a short-term opportunity to achieve this goal.

Tax Rates, Tax Credits, and Deductions

At one time, tax rates were as high as 90 percent. Today, high tax rates are a thing of the past. Tax rates have come down over the years and recent tax rate reductions now provide a top tax rate of

35 percent. Because our tax system uses graduated tax rates, higher-income taxpayers also benefit from tax rate reductions in the lower tax brackets.

10 Percent Income Tax Bracket

There is a 10 percent tax bracket that benefits all taxpayers. For 2005 (after taking the adjustment for inflation into account), the 10 percent tax bracket applies to:

- The first $7,300 of taxable income for single individuals.
- The first $10,450 of taxable income for heads of households.
- The first $14,600 of taxable income for married couples filing joint returns.

Caution

The recent reduction in the regular income tax rates increases the likelihood that taxpayers will be subject to the AMT. The reason: As the regular tax declines through lower tax rates and new deductions, it is more likely that AMT will exceed it, creating AMT liability. Taxpayers more susceptible to the AMT include those with significant capital gains and dividend income, and those who live in states with high state income tax rates.

Observation

The National Taxpayer Advocate reported to Congress that the number of taxpayers affected by the AMT could hit 12.5 million in 2005 and 30 million by 2010 if something isn't done. The general consensus is that Washington will have to come up with a more permanent solution to the AMT problem or suffer the political consequences. The increasing budget deficits, however, will make it very difficult to find a solution.

Observation

Generally, the creation of the 10 percent income tax bracket enhances the tax advantage of moving ordinary income such as interest over to children age 14 and older. People in the top income bracket, for example, can save 25 percent in taxes by shifting up to $7,550 in 2006 in income to a child. That is the difference between the 10 percent bracket and the top 35 percent bracket. As explained later in this chapter and in more detail in Chapter 2, shifting capital gains and dividends to low-bracket children also can be advantageous. (Be careful about this, however, because the unearned income of children under age 14 in excess of $1,600 is taxed under the so-called *kiddie tax* rules at the parents' marginal tax rate.)

Upper-Income Individuals Won't Lose Deductions

After 2005, the overall limitation on itemized deductions, which now reduces the value of certain itemized deductions claimed by higher-income individuals, is scheduled to be phased out. In effect, higher-income individuals will have a small tax rate reduction.

In 2005, itemized deductions—except medical expenses; casualty, theft, or gambling losses; and investment interest expense—are reduced by 3 percent of the individual's AGI above $145,950 for unmarried people as well as married couples filing joint returns ($72,975 for married individuals filing separately). Although these amounts are adjusted annually for inflation, this rule can cause you to lose as much as 80 percent of itemized deductions in this category.

In 2006, the 3 percent reduction drops to 2 percent. The reduction falls to 1 percent in 2008, and is eliminated in 2010. In 2006, the phase-out begins at AGI of $150,500 ($75,250 married filing separately).

Personal Exemptions Won't Be Lost

The reduction of personal exemptions that is now imposed on higher-income taxpayers is phased out. Beginning after 2005, those affected will receive what is, in effect, an additional tax rate reduction.

Currently, deductions for personal exemptions ($3,200 each in 2005) are reduced or eliminated at higher income levels. For 2005, the deduction must be reduced by 2 percent for each $2,500 ($1,250 for married people filing separately) or a portion of $2,500 that the taxpayer's AGI exceeds $218,950 for joint returns; $109,475 for married couples filing separately; $182,450 for heads of households; and $145,950 for single individuals. For 2005, personal exemptions are completely phased-out at $343,750 on joint returns; $171,975 for married individuals filing separate returns; $307,450 for heads of household; and $270,950 for single individuals (see Chapter 14 for 2006 figures).

The personal exemption phase-out will be reduced by one-third for 2006 and 2007, two-thirds for 2008 and 2009, and eliminated altogether after that.

Alternative Minimum Tax

The AMT was intended to ensure that high-income taxpayers who benefit from various deductions, credits, and exemptions pay at least a minimum amount of tax. The AMT is calculated by reducing or eliminating the tax benefits that have been claimed for regular income tax purposes. Next, the exemption amount is subtracted, and the AMT tax rates (26 percent up to $175,000 and 28 percent above that amount) are applied to the balance. The taxpayer then compares the result with his or her regular tax and pays the higher amount. The AMT exemption is available for taxpayers with relatively modest incomes. For 2005, the exemption amount is $58,000 for married couples filing jointly and $40,250 for single taxpayers.

The exemption phases out for married taxpayers with AMT between $150,000 and $382,000. For single taxpayers the phase-out is between $112,500 and $273,500. The AMT tax rates remain at 26 percent for the first $175,000 of AMT income ($87,500 for married individuals filing separately) after the exemption, and 28 percent for the balance.

Example

The following example illustrates how taxpayers with only regular income (not capital gains or dividends) will pay more AMT merely because the regular tax rates have been reduced: See Chapter 2 for the impact of capital gains and dividend income on AMT liability.

Investment Income

The top rate on most capital gains remains 15 percent. This rate also applies to qualified dividends.

Long-Term Capital Gains

For sales and exchanges of capital assets and for installment-sale payments received after May 5, 2003, the rates are:

- 15 percent for those in regular tax brackets above 15 percent.
- 5 percent (zero, in 2008) for those in the 10 or 15 percent rate brackets.

The rates apply to capital assets held for more than one year. They apply both for regular tax and AMT purposes: 28 percent rate applies on collectibles and the taxable portion of gain on qualified small business stock, and a 25 percent rate applies to depreciation recapture on the sale of buildings for taxpayers in higher tax brackets.

After 2008, the tax rates on long-term capital gains revert to the previous 20 percent rate (10 percent for those in the two lowest tax brackets). Also, the special capital gains rate for assets held more than 5 years of 18 percent (8 percent for those in the two lowest tax brackets) again applies.

Reduced Dividend Rates

Qualified dividends received by individuals are taxed at the same rate as the tax on capital gains, or 15 percent (5 percent for individuals below the 25 percent tax bracket). The reduced rates on dividends apply through December 31, 2008.

Caution

To qualify for the special rate on dividends, stock must be held for more than sixty days during the 121-day period that begins sixty days before the ex-dividend date in order for a dividend to qualify for the preferential rates. For dividends paid on preferred stock that represent payments of dividend arrearages in excess of one year, however, the required holding period is 90 days during the 181-day period that begins 90 days before the ex-dividend date. The holding period is extended by any days on which the shareowner has diminished the risk of loss through options or other means.

Not all dividends qualify. Dividends paid by mutual savings banks, exempt organizations, and farmers' co-ops don't qualify for the reduced rates. Nor do dividends that the shareholder is obliged to pay to someone else, such as in connection with a short sale. Nor do dividends that the shareholder elects to treat as investment income against which investment interest may be deducted qualify. If a shareholder receives an extraordinary dividend that qualifies for the capital gains tax rates, any loss on the dividend-paying stock is a long-term capital loss to the extent of the extraordinary dividend.

Dividends from Pass-Through Entities

Qualified dividend income passed through from partnerships and bank common trust funds qualifies for the preferential capital gains rates. Qualified dividends passed through from mutual funds and real estate investment trusts (REITs) also generally qualify for the capital gain rates. However, certain distributions that generally are called dividends but really are not—such as life insurance policy dividends and money market fund dividends—do not qualify.

Observation

The current law capital gains and dividend rates give investors a unique opportunity to reposition their portfolios and seek an allocation of investment assets that is better diversified and more consistent with their risk tolerance. Investors can sell their appreciated assets at a low tax rate of 15 percent and then reinvest the proceeds in a diversified portfolio of securities that can earn a higher rate of return for the level of risk assumed. Preferred stock with a high dividend yield and other income stocks can now be more effectively combined with a portfolio of growth and value stocks to produce a more predictable after-tax rate of return now that dividends and capital gains are taxed at the same rate.

Estate Taxes

The estate tax law changes that were expected to be enacted this Fall have been put on hold by Congress due to the impact of hurricane Katrina. As a result, the following discussion summarizes the current state of the federal estate tax system:

- The changes in the so-called "death tax" over the past several years have created considerable estate planning complexities for the wealthiest 2 percent of taxpayers—those who may owe estate taxes on their accumulated wealth when they die. The amount that can be passed at death free of federal estate tax has grown so that many may think that they no longer need to be concerned with estate tax planning. However, planning is still vital. First, federal estate tax cuts (culminating in no estate tax in 2010) are temporary. After 2010, old estate tax rules are poised to take hold again. In addition, state death tax rules may now apply to estates that might otherwise have escaped this level of taxation. No doubt, there will be more changes ahead.

Observation

The estate tax exemption amount, which is currently $1.5 million per person, is scheduled to increase to $2 million per person beginning January 1, 2006. Individuals will need to consider whether their current estate disposition plans and documents will appropriately deal with this additional exemption amount.

The estate tax—and another death tax called the generation-skipping transfer (GST) tax—began to phase-out starting in 2002, and are scheduled to be eliminated entirely in 2010. The gift tax is not scheduled to be repealed, but its effect has been reduced under certain circumstances. As with the income tax provisions, all of the estate and gift tax changes are scheduled to sunset after 2010. Therefore, the repeal of the estate tax will last for only one year (2010) unless Congress makes further changes that are signed into law. Accompanying the repeal of the estate tax are some income tax changes that may cause appreciation in some of a decedent's property to be subject to income tax. Currently, appreciation in property that occurred during a decedent's life escapes capital gains taxation. These scheduled changes should cause many people to reconsider and revise their estate plans.

Phase Down of the Estate Tax

The gradual repeal of the estate tax is accomplished by:

- Increasing the amount that is shielded from estate tax.
- Reducing the top estate tax rate.

Exemption Increases

The estate tax exemption amount in 2005 is $1.5 million. There-after, the exemption amount increases gradually to $3.5 million in 2009 for estate tax purposes. The gift tax exemption amount remains at $1 million. The GST exemption amount is the same as the estate tax exemption amount (e.g., $1.5 million in 2005).

Observation

The annual gift tax exclusion has not been changed by recent tax acts, but is adjusted annually for inflation. For 2006, the limit has increased by $1,000 to $12,000 ($24,000 for couples who agree to split the gift).

Rate Reduction

The highest estate and gift tax rate—which had been 55 percent in 2001—is 47 percent in 2005. It will decline by 1 percent a year to 45 percent in 2007.

Beginning in 2010, the top gift tax rate is scheduled to decline to 35 percent, which is the same as the top individual income tax rate. The estate, GST, and gift tax rates and exemptions, from now through 2011, are represented in Table 1.1.

Table 1.1 Year-by-Year Transfer Tax Rates and Exemptions				
	Exemption (in $ Millions)			**Highest Estate, GST, and Gift Tax Rate**
Year	**Estate Tax**	**GST Tax**	**Gift Tax**	**(%)**
2005	1.5	1.5	1	47
2006	2	2	1	46
2007	2	2	1	45
2008	2	2	1	45
2009	3.5	3.5	1	45
2010	N/A (taxes repealed)	N/A (taxes repealed)	1	35 (Gift tax) 0 (Estate and GST tax)
2011 and later	1	1.12 (indexed)	1	55

Caution

The increased estate tax exemption requires taxpayers to reexamine their estate plans if their wills and those of their spouses contain bypass or credit-shelter trusts, which many wills do to ensure that both spouses' estates use the full estate tax exemption amount. These bequests are intended to leave the maximum amounts that can be passed on to children or other heirs (or in trusts for their benefit) without incurring estate tax. As the exemption increases, these arrangements will be funded with larger and larger amounts, and possibly all of a decedent's assets, sometimes leaving nothing for the surviving spouse.

Loss of Credit for State Death Taxes

In the past, federal estate tax could be offset by a credit for state death taxes paid at a decedent's death. The credit could have been approximately 16 percent of the estate. In 2005, however, the state death tax credit is repealed and replaced by a deduction for those taxes actually paid to any state.

Observation

The credit has been an important source of revenue for many states. Some states have enacted their own estate taxes to compensate for the repeal of this credit and others are considering similar actions, a factor that should be considered when people decide where to live in retirement.

Loss of Full Basis Step-Up

Repeal of the estate tax in 2010 will be accompanied by the repeal of the present income tax rules, which provide that a beneficiary's basis (the cost used to figure the gain when property is sold or otherwise disposed of) in assets, acquired from a decedent, is generally "stepped-up" to fair market value as of the date of death. This basis step-up eliminates capital gains tax liability on appreciation in inherited assets that occurred during the decedent's lifetime. Those who inherit property from decedents who die in 2010, however, will receive only a limited basis step-up, which will eliminate income tax on a maximum of $1.3 million of gain that accrued during the decedent's life. Property inherited by a surviving spouse will get an additional $3 million of basis increase, thereby allowing a total basis increase of up to $4.3 million for property transferred to a surviving spouse. (If the decedent was a nonresident alien, the aggregate basis increase would be limited to $60,000, regardless of the beneficiary's relationship to the decedent.)

In addition to the allowable basis step-up, an estate or its beneficiaries who acquire the principal residence of a decedent who dies in 2010 will be able to qualify for tax-free treatment on its sale if that decedent could have qualified. The result can be an additional income tax-free gain of a maximum of $250,000.

The estate's executor will choose which of the decedent's assets will receive the basis increase. (There will be a number of restrictions on basis allocation to avoid the creation of artificial tax losses and other effects not intended by the rule.) Certain additional basis increases will be permitted so that the decedent's losses that were not deducted are not wasted. After permitted basis increases have been exhausted, beneficiaries will receive a basis in the property equal to the decedent's adjusted basis (referred to as a carryover basis) or the fair market value of the property on the date of the decedent's death, whichever is less. For property owned jointly by spouses, only the decedent's half of the property will be eligible for a basis increase.

Donors and estate executors will be required to report information about certain transfers to the IRS and to donees and estate beneficiaries, including basis and holding period information.

Observation

The executor will be responsible for allocating the aggregate basis increase limits among different assets and various beneficiaries of the property. If some beneficiaries receive higher basis property, the other beneficiaries may be burdened with higher capital gains if they sell the inherited property.

Estate planning may help minimize the potential for family strife or litigation over basis allocation issues after a benefactor's death.

Caution

Only property transferred outright to the surviving spouse or held in a special form of trust known as a *qualified terminable interest property* (QTIP) trust qualifies for the additional $3 million of basis increase for property passing to surviving spouses. Many persons now have testamentary plans in which bequests to surviving spouses are held in other forms of trusts that qualify for the marital deduction for estate tax purposes, but won't qualify for the $3 million basis increase.

Observation

For those interested in charitable giving, retirement assets are an excellent choice of assets to leave to charity. Because retirement assets do not qualify for a step-up in basis either currently or after the repeal of the estate tax, and generally, don't even qualify for capital gains tax rates, income tax consequences can be minimized by leaving the retirement assets to charity rather than other property or cash.

Qualified Domestic Trusts

A *qualified domestic trust* (QDOT) qualifies for the estate tax marital deduction when the surviving spouse is not a U.S. citizen. Generally, the estate tax is deferred until the death of the surviving spouse, at which time an estate tax based on the value of the trust principal that remains must be paid. If distributions of trust principal are paid out to the surviving spouse before death, estate tax also would be payable based on the value of those distributions. The QDOT principal escapes estate taxation if the surviving spouse dies in 2010. However, any distribution of principal from a QDOT to a living spouse will remain subject to the estate tax through 2020, but would be free of estate tax in 2021. However, because 2021 will occur after the December 31, 2010 sunset date, the 2001 Tax Act in effect, voids this provision.

Observation

It is possible to avoid estate tax entirely in the case of QDOTs that are established before 2010. QDOTs, therefore, should be considered when planning the estate of anyone married to a non-U.S. citizen.

Installment Payment of Estate Taxes

To alleviate the liquidity problems of estates comprised significantly of closely-held business interests, qualifying estates may defer the estate tax attributable to a closely held business on an installment basis for up to 14 years at a low interest rate.

Observation

This provision provides additional relief for an often-overlooked issue of estate planning: ensuring sufficient liquidity to pay estate taxes. Recent changes liberalized the rules so that additional businesses can qualify for this relief. However, they must still comprise at least a certain minimum percentage of the total estate assets; other requirements apply as well.

What's Next?

In this chapter, we explained the significant tax changes impacting individuals in 2005, and reviewed the current estate tax rules. Now it is time to discuss in detail how taxpayers should handle their investments to take advantage of new opportunities in light of the current law tax rates on dividends and capital gains. Although people who profit from investments generally must hand over some of their gains to the government in the form of taxes, no one has any obligation to pay any more than is legally due, and it is as wise as it is legitimate to plan an investment strategy to take maximum advantage of what is provided in the tax law.

Chapter 2

INVESTMENTS AND STOCK OPTIONS

During the years 2000 through 2002, investors were more worried about their investment losses rather than the taxes they would have to pay on investment gains. In 2003, the stock market rebounded sharply. Since 2003, stock market gains have been moderate. During this time, investors have been rewarded with reduced regular tax rates for interest and short-term gains, and even lower rates for long-term capital gains and dividends. These changes should attract the attention of every investor, whether they invest in stocks, bonds, sophisticated hedge funds, or simple certificates of deposit. However, the changes are not permanent. The reduced regular tax rates are scheduled to apply only through 2010, and the new capital gains and dividends rates apply only through 2008. Clearly, it is imperative for investors to continuously monitor their portfolios in light of the ever-changing tax regulations to maximize their after-tax rate of return.

Under current tax regulations, individual income tax brackets are adjusted for inflation annually. As these adjustments occur, investor tax liability is reduced on investment income subject to ordinary income rates, such as interest and short-term capital gains. Long-term capital gains and dividends are taxed more favorably. They are subject to a maximum tax of only 15 percent. For those in the two lowest tax brackets—such as many children and grandchildren—the rate is a mere 5 percent and, for 2008, it will be zero!

Investors must also consider the effect of the alternative minimum tax (AMT) on any market gains. The after-tax benefit from investing in municipal bonds, for instance, may be lessened for investors who are subject to the AMT. Even though the reduced capital gains and dividends tax rates apply for AMT as well as regular income tax purposes, these types of income can nonetheless help trigger the AMT. The general consensus is that Washington will have to come up with a more permanent solution to the AMT problem or suffer the political consequences. However, the increasing budget deficits will make finding a solution elusive.

Instead of investing in municipal bonds, many taxpayers will choose to convert some of their investments to Coverdell Education Savings Accounts or college tuition savings plans for their children. Others may find that the reduced tax rates on investment income favor other saving strategies. We describe these strategies in depth in Chapter 5.

Investors should also take note that the phasing out of the estate tax has a "Catch-22" clause that should impact their investment decisions: In 2010, securities and other capital assets held in an estate at death will no longer escape all capital gains tax when passed on to heirs. Under the new law, the heirs' tax-free gains on inherited property will be limited to a *total* of $1.3 million. An additional $3 million of gains on property received by a surviving spouse will also escape capital gains tax. Until now, many investors have assumed that securities with very large gains should be retained until death for heirs in order to receive a tax-free step up in basis. In some instances, that strategy may not be appropriate as a result of the limit on capital gains that can pass to heirs tax-free in 2010.

In this chapter, we discuss in detail the many ways taxpayers can maximize their investment options on an after-tax basis under today's tax regulations. Particular attention is paid to making the best tax use of capital losses. We include a checklist of ideas to consider as you plan your investment strategies for the decade to come.

Capital Gains

Capital gain income results when a taxpayer sells or exchanges a capital asset that is held for longer than one year. Examples of capital assets include shares of stock or securities, a personal residence, or a work of art.

Favorable Rates

The rate on long-term capital gains (gains from assets held for more than one year) is currently only 15 percent.

Example

In April 2005, an individual in the top ordinary income tax bracket (35 percent in 2005) sold stock that he purchased over a year earlier, recognizing a gain of $10,000. His long-term capital gains tax is $1,500—15 percent of $10,000.

Observation

The reduced tax rates on long-term capital gains make stock investments more advantageous over shorter holding periods, and reduce the attractiveness of "ordinary income" investments, such as regular IRAs (but not Roth IRAs), tax-deferred annuities, and fixed income investments.

Observation

The capital gains rate effectively increased for taxpayers in high tax brackets through the itemized deduction cutback and the personal exemption phase-out (see Chapter 8). The loss of

(continued)

Continued

personal exemptions and phase-out of itemized deductions will be less of a problem in the future, when the phase-outs of these write-offs are gradually reduced, beginning in 2006. For now, the marginal tax rate on net long-term capital gains for higher-income taxpayers may be 22 percent or higher, depending on personal circumstances.

Exceptions to the 15 Percent Rate

Individuals in the 10 percent or 15 percent ordinary income tax bracket have a long-term capital gains rate of only 5 percent. For sales in 2008, there is no tax on these gains.

Example

Assume your 19-year-old daughter's regular income (from wages and interest) is taxed at no more than 15 percent, and she sells stock that she purchased over a year ago for a gain of $10,000. Her capital gains tax is only $500 (5 percent of $10,000).

Observation

The availability of the 5 percent rate for those in the lowest two tax brackets presents a great family income-splitting opportunity. Higher-income tax bracket parents can transfer stock or other capital assets held to their lower-income tax bracket children or grandchildren. The children or grandchildren can, in turn, sell the assets (but not before the year they turn 14 or the "kiddie tax" will kick in) and qualify for the lower 5 percent rate to the extent the gains do not push their income above the 15 percent bracket (taxable income of $29,700 for singles in 2005). The holding period for the asset transferred carries over to recipients of the property when the gift is made. As a result, the transfer results in a 10-percentage-point tax savings.

Example

An individual in the top tax bracket (35 percent in 2005) owns stock purchased more than one year ago on which he has a $10,000 gain. If he sold the stock in 2005 to help pay for his grandson's college tuition, for example, his long-term capital gains tax would be $1,500 or 15 percent of $10,000. If he gives the stock to his 17-year-old grandson, who has only a few thousand dollars of taxable income this year from a summer job, the tax bill would be only $500 on his grandson's sale of the stock, saving $1,000.

A higher maximum tax rate of 28 percent applies to long-term capital gains from the sale of collectibles (such as art or antiques), and to one-half of the long-term capital gains from the sale of qualified small-business stock (the other half of the gain on the sale of such stock, up to certain limits, is tax-free). Furthermore, there is a 25 percent tax rate on part of the gain resulting from the sale of real estate where depreciation deductions were previously taken.

Example

An individual who is not an art dealer sells an oil painting from his personal collection, which he has owned for many years, for $100,000 more than he paid for it. His capital gains tax liability is $28,000 or 28 percent of $100,000.

Observation

The 15 percent rate on long-term capital gains and dividends is set to run only through 2008, so investors with unrecognized gains may want to evaluate selling assets now in order to take advantage of the current low rate. Of course, investors will want to compare the prospective tax savings to the future appreciation potential for the investment before making any decision.

No More Advantage for Five-Year Gains

There has always been a required minimum holding period to qualify for long-term capital gains rates. Over the years, it has varied from more than six months to more than two years. Before May 7, 2003, there was a separate holding period for special capital gains rates. The rate was an 18 percent rate (or 8 percent for those in the two lowest tax brackets)—for certain capital assets held more than five years:

- **18 percent rate.** This rate would have applied to sales of property held for more than five years if the holding period for the property began in 2001 or later.

- **8 percent rate.** This rate would have applied to sales of property held for more than five years and sold in 2001 or later. There was no requirement for the holding period to have begun after 2001 to qualify for this low rate.

These special rates have been repealed for now. However, they should not be completely forgotten since they are scheduled to return after 2008, when the current low capital gains rates expire.

Effect of Past Election to Get the 18 Percent Rate

Investors had the opportunity to qualify assets purchased before 2001 for the 18 percent rate by electing to treat any or all of the assets as having been sold and repurchased at the beginning of 2001. Those who made this election for readily tradable stock were deemed to have sold and repurchased it at its closing price on the first business day after January 1, 2001. The deemed sale and repurchase of other capital assets, such as real estate or artwork, was treated as made at their fair market values on January 1, 2001. By making this election, investors were able to start a new post-2000 holding period without actually going through the trouble and expense of selling and repurchasing the property.

Caution

If you made a deemed-sale election, it *cannot be* revoked, even though long-term capital gains rates have now dropped to 15 percent. Congress did not elect to allow those who previously made the election, and as a result prepaid capital gains tax at a higher rate, to go back and undo it in order to take advantage of the new 15 percent rate.

Netting Rules

Favorable capital gains rates and the long-term capital gains holding requirements may influence the decision as to when a property is sold, which in turn, effects the tax that is ultimately paid. When calculating capital gains income, keep in mind that the following ordering rules apply to netting capital gains and losses. The rules are fairly complicated, but they generally produce the lowest overall tax.

Long-term capital gains and losses (for this purpose, long-term refers to a holding period of more than one year) are divided into three groups determined by tax rates:

1. A 28 percent group (for long-term capital gains from the sale of collectibles such as art or antiques, and half of the long-term capital gains from the sale of qualified small-business stock).
2. A 25 percent group (for part of the gain from the sale of depreciable real estate).
3. A 15 percent group for all other capital assets.

For those in the two lowest ordinary income tax brackets, gains and losses in the 5 percent, 8 percent, and 10 percent groups also must be netted. Long-term gains and losses within a tax-rate group are first netted against one another. Net losses within a long-term tax-rate group are then used to offset net gains from the long-term tax-rate group with the highest tax rate. If there are net losses remaining, they offset gains from the next-highest tax-rate group.

Example

Assume that for 2005 there will be net losses in the 15 percent tax-rate group. The net losses first offset any net gains in the 28 percent tax-rate group, then offset net gains in the 25 percent tax-rate group, and finally, offset net gains in the 15 percent tax-rate group. This automatically produces maximum tax savings from the losses. Similarly, long-term capital loss carryovers offset net gains for the highest long-term tax-rate group first, then the other long-term tax rate groups in descending order.

Example

A net long-term capital loss carryover from 2004, first offsets 2005 net 28 percent capital gains, then net 25 percent capital gains, and finally, net 15 percent gains.

Net short-term capital losses offset net long-term capital gains beginning with the highest tax-rate group.

Example

A net short-term capital loss first offsets net 28 percent capital gains, then net 25 percent capital gains, and finally, net 15 percent capital gains.

Net long-term capital losses can offset short-term capital gains.

Capital Losses

Capital losses are deductible dollar-for-dollar against capital gains. In addition, you may deduct up to $3,000 in net capital losses (either short-term or long-term) each year against ordinary income (such as wages or interest income). Amounts in excess of $3,000 may be carried forward indefinitely.

Wash Sale Rule

If securities or mutual funds held have significantly declined in value and a recovery in price is not anticipated in the near future, consideration should be given to selling the securities or funds currently to take advantage of the loss. For investment reasons, there may be an ongoing desire to maintain a similar type of investment. The repurchase must be made carefully, however, so as to not immediately repurchase the same or "substantially identical" (the IRS uses this term to broaden the prohibited repurchase to securities and/or mutual funds that are not identical to what you had sold but are essentially the same) assets. Tax wash sale rules prevent a taxpayer from recognizing the tax loss if the repurchase occurs within 30 days before or after the sale of the same or substantially the same security.

If the wash sale rule is triggered, the resulting loss is suspended and added to the cost basis (the amount you pay for the security plus other acquisition costs, such as brokerage commissions). When the replacement security is sold, the suspended amount will reduce the taxable gain or increase the taxable loss.

To avoid the wash sale rule, you must either avoid purchasing the same or substantially identical assets within the 61-day period, or buy the same or "substantially identical" assets at least 31 days before or after the sale of the securities or mutual funds. Of course, the latter alternative involves substantial investment risk as the market can move against the targeted strategy in the 31-day waiting period.

> **Caution**
>
> Be careful not to trigger the wash sale rule unwittingly. A wash sale will happen, for example, if you sell *part* of your investment in a security or fund at a loss, and a dividend paid on the remaining shares is automatically reinvested in the same shares within the restricted 30-day (before or after) period.

Observation

It is always helpful to review your realized and unrealized capital gains and losses as well as loss carryovers on a periodic basis. This is especially important for future-year tax planning. If you have unrealized capital losses, consider recognizing losses to the extent of realized capital gains if it is also prudent to do so from an investment perspective. Also, you may wish to realize an additional $3,000 in losses since the incremental amount can be used to offset taxable ordinary income.

Protecting and Postponing Stock Gains

Current regulations prevent the use of the "short sale against the box" technique to safely lock in gains while postponing the taxable recognition that would occur upon the sale. Two other viable strategies remain:

1. Buying put options covering stock you own. A put option entitles the holder to sell a number of shares (usually in lots of 100 shares) of the underlying security at a stated price on, or before, a fixed expiration date. By purchasing an option to sell a security at a fixed price, any decline in the price of the security is likely to be offset, at least in part, by an increase in the price of the put option purchased.

2. Writing covered call options. A call option entitles the holder to purchase a number of shares of the underlying security at a stated price on, or before, a fixed expiration date. When a call is written, the seller of the call option receives money today in exchange for agreeing to purchase the security back at the call price in the future. As a result, the holders of a security who write a call option on the security protect their position to some extent by the proceeds from the sale of the option. More complex strategies also exist including collars and variable prepaid forwards. Additionally, by using a charitable remainder trust, capital gains can also be deferred or possibly eliminated.

Observation

The lower tax rate on capital gains should cause taxpayers to review their stock-hedging strategies. Carrying costs associated with hedging strategies that were acceptable with a 20 percent capital gains rate may be excessive with a 15 percent capital gains rate. At some point, it may make sense for taxpayers to simply pay the capital gains tax and unwind the hedging strategy. This could be particularly true for grandfathered short-against-the-box transactions where the underlying security has continued to appreciate.

Passive Activity Losses

Investment losses from business and rental activities are limited by a complex set of provisions known as the *passive activity loss rules.* In general, losses and credits from passive activities can offset only passive income and may not be used against earned income (such as salaries) or portfolio income (such as dividends or interest). Passive activities generally include any business or rental activity in which you do not materially participate. For example, renting a residence or commercial property is usually considered a passive activity.

Observation

Real estate professionals may deduct losses and credits from rental real estate activities in which they materially participate without limitation from the passive loss rules.

Consider the following year-end strategies if you have unusable passive losses:

- Purchase investments that generate passive income, to the extent the purchase is consistent with your overall investment strategy.

- Become a material participant in the activity, if feasible, by increasing your level of involvement.
- Sell or dispose of your entire interest in the passive activity to free up the losses.

Observation

Even more restrictive rules apply to certain types of passive activities such as publicly traded partnerships. Publicly traded partnership losses can offset only publicly traded partnership income, not income from other types of passive activities.

Careful Record Keeping: Identification of Securities

If you hold many securities, it is imperative to keep accurate records of your purchase history in order to maximize the tax savings at the time of sale. Because of differences in holding periods and the tax basis of individual lots, a sale can trigger a short-term or long-term gain or loss, depending on which securities are sold or are deemed to have been sold. If you redeem an actual security certificate at the time of sale, the securities sold will be those identified on the certificate. If one certificate represents securities acquired on different dates or at different prices, the specific securities to be sold can be identified to the executing broker in writing. If you do not identify specific securities, you will generally be deemed to have sold the first securities acquired, which would have the longest holding period (and therefore might be taxed at a lower rate), but may also have the largest taxable gain.

Observation

Mutual fund shares are usually treated in the same way as other securities, or you can use their average cost when determining basis. Once you apply the earliest-cost or average-cost method to a particular security, you must continue to use that method in future years.

Observation

When selling stock that has risen in value, taxes can be reduced by identifying the securities with the highest basis as the ones that are being sold. However, if the securities have been held for one year or less, any gain will be short-term, subject to tax at ordinary income rates.

Dividends

Dividends received by an individual shareholder from domestic and many foreign corporations (including American Depository Receipts or ADRs) that meet the definition of "qualified dividend income" are taxed at the same low rates that apply to long-term capital gains. This treatment applies for purposes of both the regular tax and the AMT. Thus, qualified dividends are taxed at rates of 5 percent (zero, in 2008) for taxpayers in the two lowest tax brackets, and at 15 percent for those whose income is taxed above the 15 percent tax bracket. Qualified dividend income passed through to individuals from partnerships, S corporations, limited liability companies, and trusts maintains its character as qualified dividend income and thus is taxed to individuals at the new reduced rates.

Caution

Similar to taxpayers who have been subject to AMT in the past due to high capital gains, taxpayers who now receive large amounts of dividend as well as capital gain income may find themselves subject to AMT. Taxpayers in the 28 percent, 33 percent, or 35 percent marginal tax bracket who receive dividend income may find themselves subject to the AMT due to the disparity in the rates between the AMT and the regular tax. For example, a taxpayer in the 35 percent tax bracket with $1 of dividend income would save $0.20 for regular tax purposes

(continued)

Continued

(35 percent versus 15 percent tax rate), but only $0.13 for AMT purposes (28 percent versus 15 percent tax rate). Further, the phase-out of the AMT exemption results in AMT income effectively being taxed at 125 percent of the applicable AMT rate. Thus, it is possible that a taxpayer in the AMT phase-out range will pay an effective rate of 22 percent (15 percent plus 25 percent of 28 percent) on capital gains and dividends rather than the stated AMT rate of 15 percent.

A shareowner must hold dividend-paying stock for more than 60 days during the 121-day period beginning 60 days before the ex-dividend date in order for the dividends received on the stock to be eligible for the reduced tax rates. For dividends received on certain preferred stock (generally dividends that represent an earnings period of more than one year), shareholders must hold the stock for more than 90 days during the 181-day period beginning 90 days before the ex-dividend date. These required holding periods do not include any days on which the taxpayer has reduced the risk of loss on the stock by purchasing a put, selling a call (other than a qualified covered call), executing a short sale of the stock, or having entered into a cashless collar or prepaid variable forward contract. Additionally, a taxpayer who is under an obligation to pay the dividend to another party will not receive qualified dividend income. Thus, a person with a short-against-the-box position will pay tax at ordinary rates on dividends received.

If an individual receives an extraordinary dividend eligible for the reduced rates, any loss on the sale of the dividend-paying stock is treated as a long-term capital loss to the extent of the dividend. (A dividend on preferred stock is treated as extraordinary if it equals 5 or more percent of the shareholder's adjusted basis in the preferred stock; a dividend on common stock is treated as extraordinary if it equals 10 percent or more of the shareholder's adjusted basis in the common stock.) Clearly, these rules make it more difficult for taxpayers to convert short-term capital gains into dividend income taxed at lower rates. However, taxpayers who have short-term capital gains, and no potential long-term capital gains or losses, could use extraordinary dividends to avoid the higher tax on short-term capital gains. The taxpayers would still have to meet the holding period requirements described earlier.

Mutual Funds and REITs

Mutual funds generally are able to pass through qualified dividend income received to the fund's shareholders where the qualified dividend will be taxed at the reduced rates. However, other types of income received by a mutual fund, such as interest received on notes or bonds, or short-term capital gain, are not qualified dividend income, even though the payments are made to mutual fund shareholders in the form of a dividend. Therefore, money market fund dividends, which represent interest earned by the money market fund, are not qualified dividend income.

Dividends paid by a real estate investment trust (REIT) generally are not eligible for the reduced dividend rates. However, dividends received by a REIT shareholder will be considered qualified dividend income to the extent that the REIT had net taxable income in the preceding year.

Observation
Mutual funds and REITs will advise shareholders as to whether the distributions are qualified dividend income eligible for the reduced tax rates.

Preferred Stock

Whether dividends on preferred stock qualify for the reduced dividend tax rates depends on the classification of the preferred stock. If the preferred stock pays a dividend from corporate earnings and profits and the preferred stock is considered a stock, then the dividend will be taxed at no more than 15 percent. If, however, the preferred stock is considered a debt instrument, its "dividend" will continue to be taxed at ordinary income rates. Since many preferred stocks are bonds in disguise, their dividends will not be eligible for the 15 percent rate.

Impact on Short Sales

A short sale is the sale of a security that is not currently owned. When a dividend is paid on stock that has been shorted before the date the short sale is closed, the short seller must pay to the lender of the shares an equivalent amount in lieu of that dividend. In general, these "in lieu of" payments are treated as interest paid for the use of the property borrowed for use in the short sale.

Once the borrowed stock or securities have been sold pursuant to a short sale, neither the short seller nor the lender retains any ownership interest in the stock, therefore the "in lieu of dividend" payment made to the lender of the stock by the seller is not a "dividend" in the sense of being a distribution made by the corporation with respect to its stock. As such, "in lieu of dividend" payments do not qualify for the reduced rates.

Impact on Margin Accounts

In the past, investors may not have known or cared whether their stock was borrowed and they were receiving "in lieu of dividend" payments rather than actual dividends. Now, however, if a dividend is considered an "in lieu of dividend" payment, the lower dividend tax rates will not be available. As a result, margin accounts have a potential tax disadvantage, since most agreements governing margin accounts specifically allow for the borrowing of shares held in a margin account.

Impact on Foreign Tax Credit

Special rules apply in determining a taxpayer's foreign tax credit limitation for qualified dividend income. Because qualified dividends now receive preferential tax treatment in the United States, dividends taxed overseas will need to be adjusted accordingly when the foreign tax credit is computed.

Impact of Reduced Tax Rates on Investment Allocation

An investor's asset allocation should be revisited in light of the current low rates on qualified dividends and capital gains including the decision as to what investments should be in which type of account, either a taxable or tax deferred account. There is no simple answer as to which investment is the most beneficial in each type of account. Clearly, consideration should be given to the character of the expected investment return produced by the investment—short- or long-term capital gain, nontaxable or taxable ordinary income, the expected portfolio turnover, the expected return on the asset class, and the time period of tax deferral.

Historically, investments producing significant amounts of taxable income each year (taxable interest or dividends, short-term capital gains, or ordinary income) would have primarily been allocated first to tax-deferred or tax-free accounts. So too would investment styles with significant portfolio turnover. Additionally, long-term capital gain assets with little portfolio turnover would have primarily been allocated first to taxable accounts.

Now, taxpayers with long-term tax deferral opportunities may be well advised to put their highest potential earning assets in tax-deferred accounts even if the withdrawal will be taxed at a rate much higher than the 15 percent current tax rate. Tax-deferred compounding on high-growth-rate asset categories for long periods of time can more than offset the benefits of low current tax rates.

Taxpayers with shorter-term tax-deferral opportunities generally should place more emphasis on the current tax rates (and tax efficiencies) when making asset allocation decisions. Shorter periods of tax deferral may not justify the loss of lower rate earnings.

Tax-Exempt and Taxable Bonds

Most interest earned on bonds is subject to tax at ordinary income rates. In most interest rate environments, bonds paying tax-exempt interest are only appropriate for investors in higher income tax brackets (federal and state). However, depending on the date on which the bond matures and the current market conditions, some long-term municipal bonds may produce a higher after-tax yield even in the 15 percent bracket (see Chapter 9). The decision is driven by the interest rate differential between taxable and tax-free bonds, assuming similar maturity and credit quality. It is important to take into account the state tax implications as well as most investments in tax-exempt investments issued by a political subdivision in a state other than the state of residence subject the taxpayer to state income tax even though the interest is free from federal tax.

Observation

Lower tax rates impact the relationship between tax-exempt and taxable bonds and will reduce the attractiveness of tax-exempt bonds, everything else being equal. Recently, since the federal tax rates have declined and tax brackets have been adjusted upwards for inflation, allowing more income to be earned without pushing a taxpayer into a higher tax bracket, tax-exempt bond issuers are being forced to raise the interest rate on their bonds to remain competitive with similar quality taxable bonds.

Taxable "Tax-Exempt" Bonds

Certain bonds (private activity bonds) are tax-exempt for regular income tax purposes but are taxable for the AMT. As a result, private activity bonds typically carry a slightly higher interest rate than bonds that are exempt from both regular tax and the AMT.

Observation

The demand for private activity municipal bonds should decrease going forward since many more taxpayers are now subject to the AMT.

Observation

If it is unlikely that a taxpayer will be subject to the AMT now or in the future, consideration should be given to private activity bonds in order to obtain the higher interest rate.

Caution

Just because a taxpayer may not have been subject to the AMT in the past does not mean that the taxpayer will not be subject to the AMT in future years. Unlike regular income tax rates, AMT rate brackets and exemption amounts are not indexed annually for inflation. AMT liability, therefore, has been affecting more and more taxpayers, many of whom consider themselves in the middle class and thought the AMT was only a tax that the wealthy paid. In 2005, AMT relief has been provided in the form of slightly increased exemption amounts. This increased exemption amount, however, is only temporary.

Legislative Alert

Congress may continue higher AMT exemption amounts and/or permit certain personal credits to offset AMT liability.

Bond Premium or Discount

Investors who pay more than face value to purchase a bond are said to have purchased the bond at a premium. Bonds purchased at a premium usually carry a higher rate of interest than the prevailing rate for newly issued comparable bonds at the time of purchase. Taxpayers who own bonds purchased at a premium must amortize the premium of a tax-exempt bond by reducing its basis over time, although for taxable bonds, a taxpayer can elect to amortize the premium by offsetting the premium against the bond's interest. If taxpayers elect to amortize the bond premium, they must do so for all bonds owned currently and later acquired. If the premium is not amortized over the bond's life, a loss will typically result when you sell or redeem the bond.

If a bond is purchased at a discount from its original issuer, the difference between the issue price and the redemption price (called "original issue discount," or OID) is considered interest income. In almost all cases, a portion of this interest must be included in income each year, even though the income is not received until the bond is redeemed. Taxable OID bonds, therefore, are best suited for purchase in tax-deferred accounts, such as IRA or 401(k) accounts, or tax-exempt accounts such as Roth IRAs.

The original issue discount rules do not apply to U.S. savings bonds, notes that mature in one year or less, or tax-exempt bonds (unless the bonds have been stripped of their coupons). If a taxable bond is purchased with a market discount—that is, a bond that has lost value since its issue date (usually because interest rates have risen since the time of issuance)—the resulting gain on sale will, in most cases, be considered interest income to the extent of the accrued market discount. The market discount must be accrued and recognized as ordinary income upon sale. If the bond is sold at a price in excess of the accrued discount, the excess is capital gain. Unlike the rule for taxable bonds, all of the market discount on municipal bonds is treated as ordinary income to the extent of the gain on the disposition of the municipal bond.

Florida Intangibles Trust

If a taxpayer is a Florida resident and pays a significant amount of Florida intangibles tax each year, he should consider establishing a Florida Intangibles Trust or other vehicle that may exempt the value of the taxpayer's intangible assets from the tax. Note that the tax rate for the Florida intangibles tax has been reduced significantly in the past few years and has been cut in half for 2006. The intangibles tax is imposed at the rate of only 0.05 percent ($1 per $2,000 of intangible assets subject to the tax).

> ### Observation
> Include the cost of establishing and operating the Florida Intangible Trust or other vehicle when determining whether this type of strategy makes sense for you.

Nonqualified Stock Options

Nonqualified stock options generate compensation income at the time the options are exercised. The compensation income equals the difference between the fair market value of the stock at the time of exercise and the exercise price. Subsequent appreciation in the value of the stock is taxed at favorable capital gains rates. Most individuals benefit by exercising nonqualified stock options shortly before the options expire, subject to the normal market risk associated with any investment decision. Early exercise, at or near the strike price, eliminates the downside protection afforded by stock options. By holding off on exercise until the latest point possible, a taxpayer will benefit from the presumably increased stock value without actually making a cash investment in the stock.

However, if the appreciation potential of the stock is expected to be great, early exercise can be advantageous because it minimizes the portion of the gain that will be taxed as compensation (at ordinary income rates) and maximizes the amount that will qualify for capital gains rates. The decision about when to exercise options should also take into account the amount of appreciation to date, the future prospects of the company, and, most importantly, the taxpayer's unique tax and investment position. Some option plans permit a taxpayer to pay the exercise price in the form of existing shares, thereby eliminating the need to fund the exercise with cash.

Withholding of federal income tax, Social Security, Medicare, and state and local taxes are all due when the options are exercised. If the stock option is exercised and then sold quickly, the cash generated from the sale can be used to help satisfy these withholding obligations.

Observation

If a taxpayer intends to retain all of the stock obtained via the exercise of options, it is important to plan properly as to how to satisfy these withholding obligations. Some plans allow the use of shares to cover withholding taxes. Some employers grant "phantom" stock in connection with nonqualified options, which can help cover withholding taxes.

Incentive Stock Options

The new, lower long-term capital gains tax rates make incentive stock options (ISOs) more attractive. However, careful planning is needed to maximize the benefits of incentive stock options if the AMT is a concern.

For regular tax purposes, an ISO exercise is not a taxable event (state and local tax treatments may differ). However, at exercise, the difference between the fair market value of the stock on the date of the exercise and the exercise price is added to an individual's AMT income for the purpose of computing the AMT. Additionally, unlike nonqualified stock options, ISOs are not subject to payroll taxes at the time of exercise.

ISOs are subject to a number of requirements imposed by the Tax Code that do not apply to nonqualified stock options. For example:

- ISOs cannot be issued at a strike price lower than the value of the stock on the date the options are granted.

- ISOs cannot be exercised more than 10 years after the options are granted.

- ISOs are not transferable except at death, and during the grantee's lifetime may be exercised only by the grantee.

- ISOs must be exercised within 90 days of termination of employment in order to retain the ISO status.

- There is a $100,000 annual limit on ISO grants.

- In order to obtain favorable ISO tax treatment, the ISO stock cannot be sold within a year of option exercise or within two years of the option grant. If option stock is sold before either of these two periods has expired, the option is treated as a nonqualified option, usually resulting in compensation income to the option holder.

Observation

For taxpayers not otherwise subject to the AMT, ISO exercises should generally be timed to occur over the life of the option (usually 10 years), in order to minimize the AMT impact and to commence the one-year holding period needed to qualify for the 15 percent capital gains tax rate. If little or no planning goes into an ISO exercise, a taxpayer may be required to pay taxes earlier or in larger amounts than may be necessary.

Caution

Care should also be taken not to sell or otherwise dispose of the stock received from an ISO exercise before one year from the exercise date or two years from the grant date, whichever is later. If a sale or disposition occurs prior to one year from the exercise date or two years from the date of grant, the sale will be taxed at ordinary income rates.

Observation

Generally, it is best to exercise ISOs early in the year if the AMT is likely to be paid. The early exercise provides flexibility to sell the shares before year-end and avoid the AMT if the stock drops in value. In this case, the taxpayer will only pay ordinary income tax on the actual gain, rather than the AMT on the spread between the fair market value at exercise and the exercise price.

Idea Checklist

☑   Reevaluate your asset allocation and whether higher return, tax efficient assets should be placed in taxable or tax-deferred accounts. However, keep tax considerations secondary to investment fundamentals.

☑ Consider how reduced capital gains and dividend rates affect investment allocations among your taxable and tax-deferred accounts.

☑ Make gifts of capital assets to your low-income tax bracket children or grandchildren to take advantage of capital gains being subject to tax at only 5 percent (zero percent if not sold until 2008).

☑ Review your capital gains and capital loss positions before year-end. Try to offset capital gains with capital losses. Keep in mind the 30-day (before and after) wash sale rule.

☑ Consider reallocating some of your bond portfolio to dividend paying stock now that dividends are taxed at no more than 15 percent. Again, keep the tax considerations secondary to investment fundamentals.

☑ Make full use of $3,000 of capital loss deduction that can be used to offset your ordinary income.

☑ Determine whether tax-exempt bonds are an appropriate investment. If so, consider whether investing in "taxable" tax-exempts will improve your cash yield.

☑ Florida residents should consider ways to reduce their Florida intangibles tax liability.

☑ Executives with incentive stock options should consider how, if possible, to minimize AMT on their exercise, and should hold the shares for more than one year from exercise (and two years from option grant) to ensure qualifying their gain for the 15 percent capital gains rate.

☑ Consider whether the carrying costs associated with hedging strategies that were acceptable with a 20 percent capital gains rate are still viable with a 15 percent capital gains rate.

☑ A key goal for most taxpayers' investment strategies is to accumulate funds for retirement. Chapter 3 assesses the many ways in which the tax law provides incentives for retirement savings.

Chapter 3

RETIREMENT PLANNING

Today, most workers have much greater tax incentives to save for retirement than ever before. There are much more favorable rules for traditional IRAs, Roth IRAs, Keoghs, and corporate retirement plans. Those who can take advantage of these opportunities can lower their taxes now, while helping to ensure their comfort and financial security during retirement. The improvements are particularly welcome now, because individual retirement planning is more important than ever. With employer paid pensions becoming more rare every year and more businesses downsizing, wage earners face the prospect of financing more of their retirement with their own resources. For most people, retirement income is likely to come from three sources:

1. Tax-favored retirement plans, perhaps including defined benefit pension plans, but more likely profit sharing, stock bonus, IRA and Roth IRA, and employer-sponsored savings plans. These include 401(k), 403(b) (for teachers and employees of tax-exempt organizations), simplified employee pension (SEP) and Keogh plans (for the self-employed), savings incentive match plan for employees (SIMPLE; plans for workers in firms with fewer than 100 employees), and 457 plans for government employees.

2. A taxpayer's investments outside of tax-favored retirement plans.
3. Social Security.

Taxpayers can now increase their contributions to qualified savings plans, with workers age 50 and over permitted to make generous catch-up contributions—reaching, in some cases, as much as $5,000 a year by 2006. High-income employees who don't qualify for Roth IRAs will be able to enroll in an employer-sponsored Roth incentive savings plan, to which they contribute after-tax funds but are allowed to withdraw the money and its gains tax-free, but with no fixed schedule of required lifetime distributions. (Roth funds can even be left income tax-free to an heir.) Some lower-income workers can even get a tax credit for as much as 50 percent of the money they contribute to qualified retirement plans and IRAs, which reduces their taxes for the year of the contribution. Now that capital gains rates have dropped to 15 percent at least through 2008, taxpayers must keep in mind the benefits of capital gains tax breaks when planning for retirement. Retirement plans allow tax-free compounding of profits, but almost all payouts are taxed at ordinary income tax rates in the year they are received. Those who expect relatively high income in retirement should weigh the merits of forgoing the tax deferral, investing after-tax funds for retirement, and being taxed on sale at lower capital gains rates. However, they should not forget that the AMT could void much of the advantage. Capital gains, while not subject to AMT, can push total income into the AMT range, subjecting other income and deductions to the AMT.

Observation

Some studies have shown that lower-income individuals may actually pay more tax and have less money available to spend in retirement by contributing to 401(k) or other retirement plans. Part of the reason for this is the high marginal tax rate on Social Security income for moderate-income taxpayers (see page 81).

We believe that moderate-income taxpayers should use retirement plans and/or IRAs to save for retirement for the following reasons:

- Putting money aside in a retirement plan clearly segregates and identifies the funds for retirement, thus reducing the temptation to spend the funds for other purposes. Indeed, the penalties for early withdrawal and, in some cases, the unavailability of the funds, make it more difficult to use the funds prematurely.

- Many 401(k) plans have some portion of the employee contribution matched by the employer. The match is not available for savings outside of the plan.

- While current tax law may, under some circumstances, result in higher taxes at retirement for tax-deferred plan proceeds, it is difficult to predict personal circumstances many years in the future, and even more difficult to predict the applicable tax law.

Since most people will benefit from maximizing tax deferral on retirement savings, this chapter details valuable planning techniques and offers suggestions that can help to reduce overall tax bills and maximize income during retirement.

Employer Plans

Qualified Retirement Plans

When possible, you should think about participating in a qualified employer pension or profit-sharing plan, 401(k) plan, 403(b) plan, Keogh, or simplified employee pension (SEP) plan. Qualified plans must meet complex participation, coverage, and nondiscrimination requirements, allowing sponsoring employers to immediately deduct their contributions. Employer contributions on your behalf are not taxed to you until you receive them. Your contributions to these plans reduce your adjusted gross income (AGI) within specified limits as well as your current tax bill. This tax deferral is achieved in exchange for reduced liquidity because you give up immediate access

to the funds. However, some plans permit you to borrow up to specified allowable limits from your account, which gives you access to
some of your savings if necessary.

> ### Observation
>
> The savings incentive match plan for employees (SIMPLE) is
> available to employees of companies with 100 or fewer em-
> ployees who do not have other types of retirement plans.
> Under this type of plan, employees may defer up to $10,000
> for 2005 and 2006 (or $12,000 if age 50 or older by year-end).
> Employers that offer a SIMPLE generally must make a non-
> elective or matching contribution on behalf of each plan
> participant.

> ### Observation
>
> There is no longer a "combined plan limit," which in the past
> put a cap on contributions for highly compensated employees
> who participate in both an employer's pension plan and a
> profit-sharing plan. Now, even if you are highly compensated,
> you can accumulate larger qualified retirement plan benefits.

There are two basic kinds of qualified employer retirement plans:

1. Defined contribution plans
2. Defined benefit plans

Defined Contribution Plans

A defined contribution plan allows your company or you—or your
company and you—to contribute a set amount each year to the
plan. Contributions are set aside in an account for you and are in-

vested on your behalf. Sometimes you have the right to determine how the contributions are invested. With a defined contribution plan, you are not guaranteed a set amount of benefits when you retire. Instead, you receive the amount in the account, which depends on how much was contributed to it and how successfully the funds were invested over the years. You get a periodic statement advising you of your current account balance.

Defined contribution plan benefits are portable, so if you change jobs, you can transfer your vested benefits to an IRA or possibly to your new employer's plan. Most defined benefit pension plans, on the contrary, don't make your vested benefit available before you reach retirement age, unless your benefit is very small (in which case, the plan may cash you out).

The most common defined contribution plans are profit-sharing plans, 401(k) plans, stock bonus plans, money purchase pension plans, and employee stock ownership plans.

Bigger Contributions Allowed

The maximum contribution for 2006 increased $2,000 to $44,000 as a result of the annual inflation adjustment. The limit on compensation taken into account in figuring the contribution also increased in 2006 to $220,000 from $210,000 in 2005 as a result of the same inflation adjustment. These higher limits mean that larger contributions and benefits are possible for the more highly compensated.

In addition to the maximum dollar contribution in the prior paragraph, there are further limits based on a percentage of compensation. The maximum allocation to an individual account is 100 percent of salary. There is a 25 percent limitation on deductions for all contributions (except elective deferrals) to defined contribution plans. Thus, a sole proprietor or a one-employee corporation will be subject to the 25 percent limit.

Caution

Highly paid employees may still not be allowed to take full advantage of the increased contribution limits after nondiscrimination tests are applied.

Profit-Sharing Plans

Profit-sharing plans allow employees to share in the company's profits, usually through an employer contribution that is a percentage of compensation. Despite what the name implies, profit-sharing plans are not dependent on corporate profits for contributions to be made. Contribution levels may be changed from one year to the next. Plan participants generally do not control how the contributions are invested.

401(k) Plans

401(k) plans are defined contribution plans that are generically known as *employee thrift and savings plans.* You, as an eligible employee, elect in advance to defer part of your compensation to the plan, and sometimes your employer will match some or all of it. Neither the amount deferred, nor your employer-matching contribution, is included in your income until distributed from the plan.

A common level of employer-matching contribution is $0.50 for every $1 the employee contributes up to a set percentage limit. For example, your employer may contribute 3 percent of your compensation if you contribute 6 percent. It is like a guaranteed 50 percent first-year return on the amount you contribute each year. Your own contributions are vested immediately, but your right to keep the matching contributions depends on the plan's vesting schedule. Matching contributions must vest either all at once after no more

than three years, or at a rate of 20 percent each year starting with
the second year of service. Employer matching contributions that
were made before 2002 are permitted to vest at a somewhat
slower rate.

> ### Observation
>
> As an employee eligible for matching contributions, you
> should make every effort to contribute at least the amount
> that will entitle you to the maximum available employer-
> matching contribution.

As a 401(k) plan participant, you generally make your own investment decisions, usually by choosing among a variety of funds selected by your employer.

401(k) Contribution Limits

For 2005, the maximum amount that you can elect to defer to
a 401(k) plan is $14,000, subject to certain overall limits. Future
contribution limits will increase considerably, as shown in the
elective deferred limits chart (see Table 3.1). If you are over 50
by the end of a year, you will be allowed to make even larger
contributions. Also, contributions you can make up to the dollar

Table 3.1 *Annual 401(k) Election Deferral Limits**		Age 50 or Older ($)
Year	**Under Age 50 ($)**	**(Includes Catch-Up)**
2005	14,000	18,000
2006 and later	15,000 as indexed	20,000 as indexed

* Not more than 100 percent of compensation.

maximums are no longer limited by any set percentage of your compensation.

Observation

This means that you may contribute the maximum dollar amount to your 401(k) plan for a year, even if that amount is half, three-quarters, or even all of your salary for the year. This important change will be especially useful in boosting retirement savings of a second family earner with modest earnings. Under previous law, the amount these lower-paid individuals could contribute was very small.

Caution

Although the law now allows 401(k) deferrals of up to 100 percent of pay, this option will be available only in plans that are amended to eliminate any lower percentage of compensation limits previously specified in the plan.

Example

Sarah, who is 47 years old, reenters the workforce in 2005, on a part-time basis after a child care hiatus of 15 years. Her employer maintains a 401(k) plan, in which Sarah is eligible to participate after 3 months of service. Sarah's husband earns enough to support the family, and Sarah wants to put as much of her earnings as possible into a retirement plan on a pretax basis. Sarah expects to earn $10,000 in compensation in 2005, during the time she is eligible to make elective 401(k) deferrals. Result: If Sarah wishes to, she may contribute 100 percent of compensation to the plan. Only the annual dollar limit on 401(k) contributions (and her FICA tax liability) would reduce the amount she can contribute.

Note that even though these pretax contributions allow you to avoid immediate income tax, they are subject to Social Security tax.

Special nondiscrimination rules apply to 401(k) elective deferrals, but those rules won't limit the catch-up contributions you make if you are age 50 or over. If your employer chooses to match catch-up contributions, the matching contributions will be subject to the usual nondiscrimination rules that apply to other employer-matching contributions.

Observation

The reductions to the tax rates for capital gains and dividends (discussed in Chapters 1 and 2) should have little impact on the decision whether to participate in 401(k) plans. The combination of tax deductions, tax-deferred accumulation, and the potential for employer-matching contributions should continue to make these plans the first-choice savings vehicle for retirement (despite the fact that distributions are subject to ordinary tax rates). There is also a psychological benefit associated with payroll deductions that makes it painless and easy to invest. Further, access to the funds prior to retirement is restricted, thus reducing the temptation to spend.

The only taxpayers who should reconsider participation are older taxpayers who are close to retirement, receive no company match, and expect to be in a higher tax bracket later.

For Small Employers

The savings incentive match plan for employees (SIMPLE) can be set up by companies with 100 or fewer employees that don't offer other types of retirement plans. As its name implies, a SIMPLE plan is easier and less expensive to set up and administer than a standard qualified retirement plan. Under this type of plan, employees may defer up to $10,000 for 2005. Employers that offer a SIMPLE generally just make a nonelective or matching contribution in the 2 to 3 percent range on behalf of each plan participant.

The contribution limits on deferrals by employees to SIMPLE plans are shown in Table 3.2.

Defined Benefit Pension Plans

Unlike a defined contribution plan, a defined benefit plan—commonly called a pension plan—pays a fixed monthly amount of income at retirement. The benefit is determined using a formula specified in the plan—usually based on your salary and the number of years you have worked for your employer. Some companies increase pension benefits during retirement to help overcome the impact of inflation.

You are entitled to your monthly pension benefit whether or not the plan contributions have been invested well. If the value of the investments falls below the amount needed to fund the promised benefit, the employer must contribute more to the plan, so you do

Table 3.2 SIMPLE Plan Maximum Deferrals*		
Year	Under Age 50 ($)	Age 50 or Older ($) (Includes Catch-Up)
2005	10,000	12,000
2006	10,000	12,500
2007 and later	10,000 as indexed	12,500 as indexed

* Not more than 100 percent of compensation.

not bear the risk of bad investments or a severe market downturn. If the plan ceases to exist, the Pension Benefit Guaranty Corporation (PBGC) pays promised benefits up to a certain level. Defined benefit plans generally do not require or allow employee contributions.

If you retire early, you will usually receive a reduced benefit, and if you work beyond normal retirement age, you receive an increased amount when you begin to collect benefits as indexed.

Increase in Benefit Limit

The maximum annual benefit that a defined benefit pension plan can fund is $170,000 in 2005 and $175,000 in 2006. This amount will be indexed for future inflation. The limit is somewhat lower for benefits beginning before age 62, and higher for payments beginning after age 65.

Nonqualified Deferred Compensation Plans

Nonqualified plans are used to reward individual executives, or other employees, without the need to treat all individuals similarly—if a company is willing to forgo current tax deductions for its contributions. (The company's deduction is delayed until the year the income is taxed to the executive.)

Observation
If you are a highly compensated employee, consider the benefits of coverage under a nonqualified plan. These plans offer the benefits of tax deferral on both the principal and the income, as well as the ability to set aside larger amounts of retirement assets than do most qualified plans.

> **Caution**
>
> The employee is treated as a general creditor of the employer
> in the event that the company enters bankruptcy. This means
> that if your employer goes bankrupt, you have to get in line
> with all the other general creditors to get a portion of your em-
> ployer's remaining assets and you may lose some or all of your
> nonqualified plan benefits.

Under a deferred compensation plan, you elect to defer a portion of
your salary or bonus until a future date (e.g., retirement). To get the
tax savings, you generally must agree to defer the compensation before the period in which it is earned or awarded.

Your Resources

Planning for retirement can include making contributions to Keogh
plans, other self-employed retirement plans such as SEPs or IRAs,
and making after-tax contributions to employer plans and 401(k)
plans if they are available to you. Make sure you maximize the tax
benefits by carefully considering the type of plan and whether contributions are deductible.

> **Observation**
>
> For most people, IRAs, simplified employee pensions (SEPs),
> and Keoghs should not be impacted by reduced tax rates on
> capital gains and dividends discussed in Chapter 2. The imme-
> diate tax deduction combined with tax-deferred growth con-
> tinues to provide an attractive after-tax potential (despite the
> ordinary income tax treatment on distributions). These ac-
> counts are particularly attractive for portfolios that produce
> significant short-term capital gains or ordinary income.

Caution

The benefits of deductible retirement savings are not as certain for taxpayers:

- Over age 70½ (only Keogh and SEP contributions are allowed for these people, but not IRA contributions).
- With an asset allocation heavy on dividend paying stocks and low portfolio turnover.
- Who expect to be in a higher tax bracket during payout.

Keogh Plans

If you are self-employed, you can maximize your retirement savings by taking advantage of self-employed retirement fund (Keogh plan) contributions. You can make a deductible contribution to your own retirement plan for a year up to the due date (including extensions) of your return. The plan itself, however, must be set up by the end of the year for which the contribution is made to take advantage of this deferred payment rule.

There are three general types of Keogh plans from which to choose:

1. **Profit-sharing plan.** Annual contributions may be discretionary, up to a certain percentage of self-employment income.
2. **Money purchase plan.** Yearly contributions based on a chosen percentage of self-employment income are mandatory.

Observation

The increased profit-sharing contribution and deduction limits generally eliminate the need to have a money purchase plan. Previously, a profit-sharing plan was often set up in tandem

(continued)

Continued

with a money purchase plan to provide the then-maximum deduction of 25 percent of compensation, while giving the employer some flexibility to alter contribution percentages if
needed. Now that the deduction limit for regular profit-sharing
plans has been raised to 25 percent, however, the mandatory
contribution required by a money purchase plan can be eliminated without giving up the ability to make 25 percent deductible contributions.

3. **Defined benefit plan.** Contributions are based on complex calculations. Although this is the most expensive kind of plan to
   operate, older, highly compensated, and self-employed individuals usually find that it permits them to make the largest tax
   deductible contributions.

Keogh contribution and deduction limits are the same as those for
other qualified retirement plans, with adjustments for the way the
self-employed's earned income is figured.

Observation

If you are self-employed and have employees, you must remember that Keogh plans are subject to complex nondiscrimination and coverage rules. You generally can't cover just
yourself if you have part-time or full-time employees who are at
least age 21 and who have worked for you for a year or more.

Simplified Employee Pension Plans

If you are self-employed or have a small company, you can also
choose to use this IRA-type plan in which a percentage of net

self-employment income is contributed to the plan (similar to a defined contribution Keogh plan). Unlike Keogh plans, simplified employee pension plans (SEPs) can be established as late as the extended tax return due date for the prior tax year. SEPs must also provide comparable benefits for employees who satisfy certain liberal eligibility requirements. Recent law changes made SEPs much more attractive by eliminating their lower 15 percent maximum contribution and replacing it with a 25 percent contribution limit to match that of other defined contribution plans. While simpler to administer than regular Keogh plans, SEPs provide fewer options than Keogh plans do for accumulating large retirement benefits, especially for older plan participants. New SEPs also cannot offer 401(k) features, such as income deferral by employees.

Traditional and Roth IRAs

Any person under age 70$\frac{1}{2}$ (or older for Roth IRAs) with at least $4,000 of earned income during 2005 can establish an IRA and contribute the maximum amount to it. There are two very different types of IRAs:

1. **Traditional IRAs.** Contributions are deductible if the IRA owner is not covered by a qualified retirement plan or if income limits are not exceeded; distributions are fully or partly taxable. Those whose income level is too high to take deductions for these contributions may make nondeductible contributions. Distributions from traditional IRAs are taxable when received and are subject to a 10 percent excise tax if taken before age 59$\frac{1}{2}$ (with certain limited exceptions).

2. **Roth IRAs.** While contributions are not deductible, earnings paid to you from these accounts are tax-free as long as certain requirements are met. Generally, the account must exist for at least five tax years, and you must receive the funds after you've reached age 59$\frac{1}{2}$, or as a result of death or disability. If

you meet the income requirements to make Roth IRA contributions, you should seriously consider doing so. Roth IRAs are an excellent retirement vehicle.

The maximum amount that you can contribute to a Roth IRA for a year phases out over an AGI range of $95,000 to $110,000 for singles, and $150,000 to $160,000 for married joint-return filers. If you are not above these income levels, you may make a contribution even if you participate in an employer-sponsored retirement plan. If your income is above these levels, you are ineligible to contribute to a Roth IRA.

Observation

Contributing to a Roth IRA is still advantageous relative to taxable investments, even after the reductions in capital gains and dividends tax rates. Roth IRAs generate tax-free income and aren't subject to the required lifetime distribution rules that govern other IRAs.

Roth 401(k)

Beginning in 2006, employers can offer Roth 401(k) accounts as an additional alternative to regular 401(k) contributions. The Roth 401(k) contributions are not deductible like regular 401(k) contributions, but can be rolled over to a Roth IRA or distributed tax-free after age 59½ and five years of participation. This feature may appeal to taxpayers who expect to be in a high tax bracket during retirement. The amount of the contribution is subject to the normal 401(k) contribution limits (see Table 3.3). To the extent you use the Roth 401(k) option, your regular deductible 401(k) contribution is reduced. It is expected that most employers will not offer the Roth 401(k) option in 2006, because of the additional complexity it creates. The Roth 401(k) is currently scheduled to sunset after 2010, and many employers are reluctant to offer a benefit option that is

Table 3.3 *Increased IRA Contribution Limits*		
Year	**Regular ($)**	**Catch-Up ($)**
2005	4,000	500
2006	4,000	1,000
2007	4,000	1,000
2008 and later	5,000	1,000

scheduled to expire in five years. Even if the Roth 401(k) is not extended, contributions made prior to expiration will be eligible for tax-free distribution.

Higher Contribution Limits

The maximum annual IRA contribution limit and catch-up contributions for those 50 or older as of the end of a year will increase, as shown in Table 3.3. The higher limit applies to both traditional and Roth IRAs.

Observation
The increase in maximum IRA contributions gives you greater opportunities to save for retirement on a tax-favored basis and will help you to rely less on employer retirement plans and Social Security.

Observation
The income limits on contributions to deductible IRAs by those who are active participants in qualified plans, eligible to contribute to a Roth IRA, or conversion of a traditional IRA to a Roth IRA have not changed. If you are a high-income taxpayer, you can make modestly larger contributions to nondeductible regular IRAs.

Observation

It makes less sense to make nondeductible contributions to a traditional IRA now that capital gains and dividend income are taxed at a maximum rate of only 15 percent, or 5 percent for those in the two lowest tax brackets, except perhaps for the fact that these rates currently are not permanent. Because capital gains and dividends that are earned within an IRA are taxed at ordinary income rates when distributed, they lose the benefit of the preferential rates. Also, funds in the IRA are subject to required distribution beginning at age $70\frac{1}{2}$, as described later in this chapter, whereas investments outside of the IRA don't have to be liquidated at any set time.

There has always been a school of thought that only long-term periods of deferral would justify the use of nondeductible IRAs (since they can convert lower tax-rate income into higher tax rate income). The reduced tax rates on dividends and long-term capital gains only add fuel to the debate. For portfolios that produce significant short-term capital gains or ordinary income, nondeductible IRAs may remain attractive, especially for those far from payout status. Also, younger taxpayers should continue to consider nondeductible IRAs, since long periods of tax deferral may overcome the other disadvantages associated with them.

One other point to consider is the implication of sunset of the lower dividend and capital gains rates in 2009, and the potential for lost IRA opportunity. If these rates are not made permanent, taxpayers who passed on nondeductible IRAs for several years will not be able to "make up" those contributions.

Traditional IRAs

Your ability to make tax-deductible contributions to a traditional IRA is limited by your income level if you are an active participant in your employer-sponsored retirement plan. The maximum deductible contribution you can make phases out over the following income levels (see Table 3.4).

If you are married, but you and your spouse file separately, your deduction phase-out range is from zero to $10,000 of adjusted gross income (AGI), effectively preventing each of you from taking IRA deductions in almost all cases in which at least one spouse is an active participant in an employer-sponsored retirement plan.

A nonworking spouse or a working spouse who is not a participant in a qualified retirement plan, but whose spouse is, has a greater opportunity to make tax-deductible contributions to a regular IRA on a joint return even though the working spouse is an active retirement plan participant. The availability of this deduction phases out for couples with an AGI between $150,000 and $160,000.

Table 3.4 *Phase-Out of IRA Deductions for Employer Plan Participants*				
	Singles and Heads of Households Deduction ($)		**Married Filing Joint Returns Deduction ($)**	
Year	**Full**	**No**	**Full**	**No**
2005	50,000	60,000	70,000	80,000
2006	50,000	60,000	75,000	85,000
2007 and later	50,000	60,000	80,000	100,000

> ### Observation
>
> If you qualify, you should always make a contribution to a Roth IRA rather than making a nondeductible contribution to a traditional IRA. No deduction is allowed in either case, but the earnings on nondeductible traditional IRA contributions will be taxed to you at ordinary income rates when you take distributions, whereas there is the potential for completely tax-free distributions from the Roth IRA. Also, there is no requirement that amounts in Roth IRAs be distributed to you during your lifetime, as there is with traditional IRAs. This allows you to keep the Roth IRA's tax shelter going for your entire life, if you so choose, and pass the tax-free earnings on to your heirs.

Conversions to Roth IRAs

Preexisting IRAs may be converted into Roth IRAs if your income is less than $100,000 (regardless of whether you are single or married). You'll have to pay income tax on these conversions, but not the 10 percent penalty that applies to early IRA withdrawals. Distributions from a Roth IRA within five years of the conversion that come from converted amounts will be subject to the 10 percent penalty tax.

> ### Observation
>
> Consider converting a traditional IRA invested in equities or stock mutual funds to a Roth IRA when stock values are depressed. The tax cost will be based on the low valuations at the time of the conversion, and no tax will be owed on future price recoveries.

> **Observation**
>
> Starting in 2005, more elderly individuals may qualify to convert their traditional IRAs to Roth IRAs. After age 70½, required minimum distributions are no longer taken into account for the $100,000 income limit on conversion eligibility.

You can change your mind and undo a conversion from a traditional IRA to a Roth IRA by transferring the funds back to a regular IRA in a direct trustee-to-trustee transfer. This will eliminate the tax liability from the conversion. You might need to do this, for example, if your AGI for the conversion year exceeds the $100,000 income limit, making you ineligible to convert. Or you may want to switch back if the value of the assets in the Roth IRA has dropped, and you don't want to pay tax on the conversion based on the higher value of the assets on the conversion date. If you convert to a Roth IRA in 2005, you will have until October 15, 2006, to transfer it back to a traditional IRA, assuming you file a timely 2005 tax return, including extensions. If you file your return before undoing the conversion, you'll need to file an amended return to report the reversal and eliminate your tax liability from the conversion.

If you have switched back to a regular IRA from a Roth IRA, you can reconvert to another Roth IRA and have your tax liability figured on the basis of the later conversion. However, you cannot reconvert until the start of the year after the original Roth IRA conversion was made, or, if later, more than 30 days after you switched the Roth IRA back to a traditional IRA.

Example

John converted a $100,000 IRA brokerage account (to which he had made only deductible contributions) to a Roth IRA in January 2005, giving him $100,000 of taxable income on the conversion.

If the value of that Roth IRA account fell to $70,000 in July 2005, John would nonetheless be liable for tax on $100,000. However, if he transfers the $70,000 directly back to a traditional IRA, he will wipe out his tax liability from the conversion. Then he can reconvert to another Roth IRA after the waiting period has passed (explained earlier), perhaps before the value of the assets in the traditional IRA has fully recovered.

Observation

When it comes to IRAs, the earlier contributions are made, the better. Take the case of a 22-year-old who contributes $2,000 annually to an IRA for just 10 years, stopping after age 31. Assuming an annual growth rate of 10 percent, the assets in that IRA will increase to approximately $895,000 by the time the IRA owner is 65 years old, even though he has contributed only $20,000 to the account.

Contrast that with a person who waits until age 32 to start contributing to an IRA, but contributes $2,000 for 33 years. The funds also earn 10 percent, but at age 65 this person's account balance is only about $540,000—that is $355,000 less than the IRA of the person who started contributing at age 22, despite $46,000 more in contributions.

Once you establish the retirement savings vehicle or vehicles that are in line with your goals (and, obviously, for which you are eligible and which are available to you), you should contribute early and regularly to benefit more fully from the effects of tax-free compounding.

Observation

You do not have to wait until you are sure of your income for a year to contribute to an IRA. You can give to either a regular IRA or a Roth IRA at any time and switch accounts by October 15 of the following year (if you have extended your tax return due date until then). For example, if you make a Roth IRA contribution or conversion during 2005, and it turns out that your income for that year is more than the allowable limit, you can transfer the funds and their earnings to a regular IRA (deductible or nondeductible, depending on your circumstances) by October 15, 2006.

Observation

Because many people in their teens and early twenties do not earn enough to save on a regular basis, this is an excellent opportunity for parents and grandparents to give their children and grandchildren a long-term gift that costs a fraction of its ultimate value. If your children or grandchildren work, consider helping them set up an IRA to capitalize on the big benefits of tax-deferred compounding (tax-free compounding with a Roth IRA) over long periods of time.

It is amazing how much the investment can grow if a contribution is made to a tax-favored retirement plan early in life. For example, if you contributed $2,000 per year for your child or grandchild while she was age 16 through 22, and never contributed another dime, assuming a 10 percent growth rate, she would have a retirement fund at age 65 of about $1.2 million, with only $14,000 in total contributions.

Observation

Giving funds to a Roth IRA for a child or grandchild will also allow the child or grandchild to withdraw $10,000 of earnings tax-free and penalty-free funds to put toward the purchase of a first home.

Tax Credit for Retirement Saving

Taxpayers with modest incomes now have another reason to save for their retirement. Through 2006, they may be eligible for a nonrefundable tax credit if they contribute to qualified retirement plans and IRAs. The maximum annual contribution eligible for the credit is $2,000 per individual. The credit is in addition to any deduction available.

For the lowest-income individuals (up to an AGI of $30,000 for joint return filers; $22,500 for heads of households; $15,000 for all others), the credit is 50 percent of the eligible contribution. That would be a $1,000 tax credit for a $2,000 contribution. The credit rate phases down from 50 percent to 10 percent of the contribution as AGI increases. It is totally phased out for those with an AGI above $50,000 for joint filers, $37,500 for heads of households, and $25,000 for singles. This credit is not available to students, taxpayers under 18, or dependents.

Observation

This credit will be available to many young taxpayers who are out of school, but whose salaries are still modest. Be sure to tell your children about the new credit and encourage or help them to get started on their retirement saving.

Charitable Remainder Trusts

Another vehicle to consider for funding a portion of your retirement is a charitable remainder trust. Although complex rules apply, funding such trusts with appreciated securities can provide an alternative to traditional qualified and nonqualified plans because they allow you to improve your cash flow on a pretax basis.

Tax-Deferred Annuities

If you have made the maximum permitted 401(k) or 403(b) contribution, contributed to an IRA, and have a decent portfolio of stocks designed to take advantage of favorable capital gains rates when the stocks are ultimately sold, you may want to consider a tax-deferred annuity. The investment earnings (usually from name-brand mutual funds and other investment alternatives) can compound tax deferred within the annuity vehicle until they are withdrawn. It is important to remember that annuities will ultimately be taxed at ordinary income tax rates (not capital gains tax rates) when distributed to you, as with a traditional IRA, even if the money is invested in mutual funds that would have been taxed at a 15 percent rate if held outside the annuity. Annuities are similar to IRAs in that there is a 10 percent excise tax generally applied to withdrawals prior to age 59. Annuities offer a guaranteed payment option that will assure a fixed level of payment for your life. You should examine the expenses and fees charged by the insurance company issuing the annuity to ensure that they are competitive with other investments. You might also consider the universal variable life insurance policy alternative discussed next.

Observation

Deferred annuities are less advantageous now that capital gains and dividend income are taxed at a maximum rate of only 15 percent—except perhaps for the fact that these rates currently are not permanent. Because capital gains and dividends that are earned within an annuity are taxed at ordinary income rates when distributed, they lose the benefit of the preferential rates. However, younger taxpayers should continue to consider annuities, since long periods of tax deferral may overcome their other disadvantages.

Split-Dollar Life Insurance

Split-dollar life insurance traditionally has been a popular tax-advantaged way to provide life insurance protection to valued employees and company owners. Split-dollar isn't a type of insurance, but rather a method of dividing the ownership and rights in a cash value life insurance policy among different parties—frequently an employer and an employee.

Under the most basic split-dollar arrangement, the employer pays most, if not all, policy premiums each year. The employee may or may not pay a portion of the premium. The employee's payment is measured by the cost of the life insurance coverage (i.e., actual term cost). If the employee did not pay, then his or her recognized income is deducted from the fringe benefit.

The employer retains the right to receive its premium advancements back from the policy proceeds at death. The employee is able to name beneficiaries for the remaining amount. The employee may actually own the policy.

If the employee owns the policy, it is known as *collateral assignment,* because the employer has a portion of the policy assigned to it as collateral for premium advancements. If the employer owns the policy, it is known as *endorsement,* because the employer endorses a portion of the death benefit to employee control.

Many complex—and advantageous—split-dollar arrangements have been developed over the years. Of particular interest to the IRS are arrangements that entitle the employee to at least some of the policy's cash value. These arrangements are known as *equity* split-dollar. The IRS concluded that the split-dollar tax rules needed to change in reaction to the widespread use of equity split-dollar arrangements.

As a result, the IRS issued some highly complex rules that it hopes capture all of the economic benefits received. These new rules will *NOT* apply to arrangements in place before September 18, 2003, and not materially modified thereafter. Thus, in theory, the new rules do not apply to preexisting split-dollar arrangements. In fact the IRS has indicated that it will apply some of the new rules to arrangements in place before September 18, 2003, that are terminated before death.

The new rules determine taxation based on who owns the policy and who pays the premiums. Endorsement arrangements will continue to be treated under historical split-dollar rules with some additional features relative to "equity" movements. For example, the nonowner of the policy will be taxed on the policy's cash value that is accessible to him. Collateral assignment arrangements will generally be treated as loans from the employer to the employee.

The new rules have also caused a reexamination of the original purpose to the arrangement as well as the policy performance. Often goals and objectives may have changed or the policy performance may have suffered due to general market conditions. In any event, the new rules make split-dollar arrangements (especially equity arrangements) more tax costly.

Observation

These split-dollar rules are now extremely complex, and anyone with an existing split-dollar arrangement or contemplating entering into one needs to get professional advice.

Universal Variable Life Insurance

Instead of a tax-deferred annuity that will be taxed on withdrawal, think about universal variable life insurance. Like its cousin, the tax-deferred annuity, the universal variable life insurance policy has an investment component consisting of mutual funds or other investment choices. The investment earnings compound on a tax-deferred basis within the life insurance policy until they are withdrawn.

One benefit is that you can borrow the investment earnings tax-free. At death, unborrowed earnings are added to the face value of the policy and can be paid to beneficiaries on a tax-free basis. You should examine the expenses and fees charged by the insurance company issuing the policy to ensure that they are competitive with similar investments.

Long-term deferral periods are needed to make the tax-free buildup overcome the "drag" on accumulations created by mortality and administration costs associated with life insurance. Since all "loaned" amounts are received income tax-free, the character of earnings within the policy is not important. Only if something goes wrong with this high-maintenance technique are income taxes triggered. When triggered, all income is subject to ordinary income tax rates (like an IRA or annuity). If something does go wrong, all the income built up in the policy is taxable at a single time—a financial disaster.

Observation

This strategy is unlikely to be undercut because of reduced rates on dividends and long-term capital gains. The strategy is to use the income tax-free nature of life insurance to build up a significant pool of assets, and then draw on that pool by "borrowing" from the policy during retirement years.

Professional Retirement Services

You and your spouse may be able to take advantage of tax-free retirement services from your employer. Your employer can provide this service as a nontaxable fringe benefit.

Observation

Retirement planning has become a very complicated, difficult process, involving important income tax, investing, estate planning, and other family-related issues. This nontaxable fringe benefit should give you better access to professionals who can help you choose the right tools and make the right decisions when considering the complex options and opportunities now available when planning for your retirement.

Social Security

If you receive Social Security payments, you may be taxed on some of the payments you receive. Benefits must be included in income if your modified AGI (which generally includes AGI, tax-exempt interest, and certain foreign-source income with other minor adjustments) plus one-half of your Social Security benefits exceeds a certain base amount. The base amount begins at $25,000 for single individuals and $32,000 for married couples filing jointly. The amount of benefits included in taxable income is the lesser of one-half of benefits received or one-half of the excess of modified AGI plus 50 percent of benefits received over the base amount. A second threshold of $34,000 for singles and $44,000 for joint returns results in more of your benefits being taxable. If this threshold is exceeded, you must include the lesser of 85 percent of benefits or the sum of the lesser of the amount included under the old rules or $6,000 ($4,500 for singles) plus 85 percent of the amount by which modified AGI, increased by 50 percent of Social Security benefits, exceeds $44,000 ($34,000 for single individuals).

Observation

The calculation of taxable Social Security benefits is not a simple one. It is often loosely stated that this provision will subject 50 percent or 85 percent of Social Security benefits to tax. In many cases, determining the amount of benefits actually subject to tax involves complicated calculations.

Observation

Because the second threshold for the tax on Social Security benefits for married filers is only $10,000 more than that for single filers, a substantial "marriage penalty" results. For example, an unmarried couple filing separately, each with total income of $37,000—$12,000 of which is from Social Security—would each be taxed on $3,000 of his or her Social Security benefits. If they were married and filing jointly, however, $20,400 of their Social Security benefits would be taxed.

Observation

The Social Security Administration now sends annual statements detailing an individual's earnings, contributions, and estimated future benefits. If you haven't received these benefit statements, use Form SSA-7004, Request for Earnings and Benefit Estimate Statement, to obtain a listing of your lifetime earnings and an estimate of your Social Security benefit. There is a limited period of time in which to correct mistakes.

Observation

The earnings limit, which previously reduced Social Security benefits by $1 for every $3 that benefits recipients age 65 through 69 earned over a certain limit, has been repealed (the earnings limit for those 62 through 65 is still in effect). As a result, those who work beyond their full retirement age no longer have their benefits reduced. However, earnings limits still apply before full retirement age (see Chapter 14).

To get information about the Social Security system, see the Social Security Administration web site, www.ssa.gov.

Required Retirement Plan Distributions

You must begin to take at least a specified minimum amount of distributions from your qualified plans and traditional IRAs by April 1 of the year after the year you turn 70½. However, if you are still working at that time and you aren't at least a 5 percent owner of your company, you do not have to begin to take distributions from a company retirement plan until April 1 of the year after you retire. If you don't take the minimum distribution, you will have to pay a 50 percent excise tax. Obviously, this is something to avoid.

> *Observation*
>
> Minimum distributions are not required from Roth IRAs during the life of the owner. This allows the tax advantages of Roth IRAs to continue until the Roth IRA owner's death and allows the income tax-free benefits to be passed to a spouse or other family member.

After years of criticism, the IRS finalized and simplified these rules. The new rules are simpler, generally spread payouts over a longer time, and give you more flexibility in naming and changing beneficiaries. You now figure your required distribution simply by dividing your account balance at the end of the previous year by a factor for your age that comes from an IRS table (see Table 3.5). You use this method even if you had been using older rules in the past. You use the same factor whether or not you have named a beneficiary, and if so, no matter how old the beneficiary is. (The only exception is if you have named your spouse as your beneficiary and he or she is more than 10 years younger than you. In that case, required distributions are based on your joint life expectancy and are even lower.)

Age	Distribution Period	Age	Distribution Period
70	27.4	93	9.6
71	26.5	94	9.1
72	25.6	95	8.6
73	24.7	96	8.1
74	23.8	97	7.6
75	22.9	98	7.1
76	22.0	99	6.7
77	21.2	100	6.3
78	20.3	101	5.9
79	19.5	102	5.5
80	18.7	103	5.2
81	17.9	104	4.9
82	17.1	105	4.5
83	16.3	106	4.2
84	15.5	107	3.9
85	14.8	108	3.7
86	14.1	109	3.4
87	13.4	110	3.1
88	12.7	111	2.9
89	12.0	112	2.6
90	11.4	113	2.4
91	10.8	114	2.1
92	10.2	115 and over	1.9

Table 3.5 *Uniform Lifetime Table for Use by Owners*

Required distributions now are almost always smaller than under the old rules. If you are taking distributions based on whom you named as beneficiary and whether you recalculate life expectancy, you are using the old, complex, and repealed rules.

> **Caution**
>
> Make sure that your required minimum IRA distribution is fig-ured using the newest rules. For most people, the amount that must be distributed is much lower than the minimum distribu-tion that was required under the old rules.

There also are now more workable rules for distributions after the account owner's death. If you have named a beneficiary, the re-maining amounts in the account are usually distributed over the beneficiary's remaining life expectancy. If you haven't designated a beneficiary, distributions can be made over a period no longer than your remaining life expectancy at the time of death. If you hadn't started taking distributions, and didn't name a beneficiary, the bal-ance remaining in your account at death would have to be paid out within five years, which doesn't afford much of a tax advantage to your survivors. As a result, it is very important that you name bene-ficiaries for your accounts and keep beneficiary designations up-dated as circumstances change.

Through post-death planning, such as use of disclaimers the post-death distribution deferral can be maximized (i.e., "stretched out"). Note that post-death estate or trust distributions cannot be used to "stretch out" distributions. If post death, your surviving spouse is the sole beneficiary of your IRA, he or she is allowed to treat it as his or her own and name new beneficiaries, which can further ex-tend the tax-deferral. However, that's generally not the case if the IRA is held in trust for your spouse.

Observation

Beneficiary designation planning can provide children or grand-children with substantial funds for tax-deferred compounding during their lifetimes. It is generally not advisable to name as the beneficiary either trusts that are not carefully structured to receive distributions or your estate.

Observation

If you continue to work past age 70½, you can hold off taking distributions from employer retirement accounts, but not from regular IRAs, until your actual retirement date, as long as you are not a 5 percent owner of the business for which the plan was established.

Observation

Roth IRAs are exempt from the rules requiring distributions to begin at age 70½. Tax-free build up can continue within a Roth IRA for your entire life. If you don't need the money during your lifetime, this can increase the amount of income tax-free accumulations in the account to pass to children and grandchildren.

Observation

Some participants in qualified retirement plans may receive favorable tax treatment if they receive a lump-sum distribution that is not rolled over to another qualified plan or IRA. Employees who receive appreciated securities of the employer as part of the lump-sum distribution from a qualified plan pay regular income tax only on the original cost of the stock (to the plan trustee). Tax on the value of the stock is at capital gains rates only when the stock is sold (capital gains from the original cost to the selling price). This special exception is known as net unrealized appreciation on employer securities. Further, employees born before 1936, may be eligible for capital gains treatment on any portion of the lump-sum that represents accumulations before 1974. The 2003 Tax Act's lower capital gains rate may encourage eligible employees to take advantage of these options.

Idea Checklist

- ☑ Maximize participation in employer plans, especially if your employer "matches" 401(k) plan contributions. Consider contributing the maximum amount permitted.

- ☑ If you are 50 or older, consider making extra catch-up contributions.

- ☑ Make your IRA contributions at the beginning of each calendar year to maximize the tax-deferred build up.

- ☑ Self-employed individuals should consider which self-employment retirement plan is best for them. Remember that Keogh plans need to be established before year-end for a tax deduction, although actual contributions can be made as late as the extended tax return due date.

- ☑ Consider reallocating investments between tax-deferred and taxable accounts to maximize tax breaks for capital gains and dividends.

- ☑ Contribute to a Roth IRA if your income level permits. This may be done even if you are in a qualified retirement plan and are not permitted to make deductible contributions to a traditional

IRA. A Roth IRA is especially desirable if you want to avoid making lifetime distributions required by traditional IRAs. Traditional IRAs have detailed distribution requirements.

☑ Consider whether converting a preexisting IRA to a Roth IRA makes sense for you and whether you can manage the tax liability generated from the conversion. This can be an especially good move when stock prices are depressed.

☑ Fund a Roth or other IRA for children and grandchildren who have earnings but insufficient cash flow to contribute to their own retirement plans.

☑ A charitable remainder trust can improve retirement cash flow if funded with highly appreciated assets.

☑ Review your beneficiary designations on retirement accounts to maximize the family's income-deferral opportunities.

The tax law makes it easier than ever for Americans to be financially secure in their later years by saving in retirement plans and IRAs. Whether all taxpayers are financially able, as well as willing, to make the change is another matter. This book is an effort to smooth the learning curve for everybody.

These retirement planning suggestions and techniques are not universally applicable; each person must pick and choose among them depending on individual circumstances. The government is providing more tax help for retirement saving, and the tax breaks stretch across the income spectrum.

We turn next to the effects of recent tax changes on home ownership. Most people do not give much thought to the federal tax implications of owning a home. They know they can deduct mortgage interest and real estate taxes, but, in fact, many other aspects of owning a home have tax consequences.

Chapter 4

TAX ADVANTAGES OF HOME OWNERSHIP

Home ownership carries with it many special tax advantages. This chapter discusses the tax considerations of home ownership in detail and explains how to use the Tax Code provisions to minimize federal tax bills. For instance, a home office has become easier to claim as a business deduction. There are tax advantages for vacation home rentals, but the rules on how to treat rental fees and expenses need careful study. Interest on limited amounts of home-equity loans is fully deductible for regular income tax purposes, regardless of how the proceeds are used. However, when calculating the alternative minimum tax (AMT), if the loan proceeds are not used for investment purposes, you can deduct home-equity loan interest only to the extent that the loan was used to improve the house. "Points" paid to secure mortgages from a bank or other lender may be treated in several ways. Finally, there are special tax breaks on gains from the sale of a house.

The 2001 Tax Act will have some interesting effects on homeowners' finances as the changes are phased in over the next decade. The 2003 Tax Act's rate cuts and capital gains tax rate reductions also will have an impact.

For instance, some married taxpayers whose itemized deductions are small may stop itemizing deductions now that the standard deduction for married couples has increased to twice that for singles. For some taxpayers, this increased standard deduction exceeds the total deductions that they could claim by itemizing. Homeowners will not complain if this happens since their total taxes will decline and their tax situation will be simplified. Some may choose to sell their homes and rent, using the freed capital for other investments.

Homeowners who continue to itemize will find their deductions worth slightly less than before the 2003 Tax Act because tax rates are lower. This will be particularly true for those who benefit by dropping out of the 25 percent bracket now that the upper limit of the 15 percent bracket has been raised for married couples to twice the size of the 15 percent bracket for singles.

A welcome recent tax law change regarding home ownership for wealthier individuals is that capital gains taxes are now lower on the profit on the sale of a principal residence that exceeds the amount that is tax-free. Before May 6, 2003, the tax on the gain in excess of $250,000 ($500,000 for married couples) was 20 percent. Now it is only 15 percent.

Techniques and tools that will help you maximize the tax benefits of owning a home are discussed in this chapter.

Tax Benefits of Owning a Home

Generally, you can deduct interest that is paid during the tax year on several types of debt related to your home or on home-equity loans, as long as they are secured by a qualified residence (your principal residence and one other home).

Mortgage Interest

You can deduct interest on debt incurred in acquiring, constructing, or substantially improving a qualified residence. Together, these debts are referred to as "acquisition indebtedness." The combined amount of debt that can be considered acquisition indebtedness is capped at $1 million.

Observation

Debt on a maximum of two residences can be counted toward the $1 million limit. Thus, if you have a city home, a beach home, and a mountain home, only debt related to your principal residence and one of the other residences can qualify as home acquisition indebtedness.

Margin interest cannot qualify as mortgage interest even where you borrow from your brokerage account to purchase a residence, because margin debt is secured by the assets in your account, not by the purchased home.

Home-Equity Loans

Interest is deductible on up to $100,000 of home-equity loans. For the interest to be deductible, the home-equity loan cannot exceed the fair market value of the residence, reduced by any acquisition indebtedness.

Interest paid on a home-equity loan is deductible in almost all situations no matter how the loan proceeds are used. For example, the fact that home-equity loan proceeds are used to finance personal expenses, such as the purchase of a new car or paying college expenses, does not generally affect interest deductibility.

Observation

Consider refinancing nondeductible personal expenditures, such as an auto loan or credit card debt, with a home-equity loan. If the tax savings from the interest deduction are used to further pay down the principal portion of the loan, the debt will be paid off sooner.

Caution

Keep in mind that home-equity interest expense is not always deductible. If the debt proceeds are used to purchase municipal bonds, for example, the interest expense is not deductible.

Vacation Homes

If your vacation home is a residence, the mortgage interest you pay is generally deductible. If your vacation home is partly your residence and partly a rental property (see the discussion that follows), your interest deduction must be prorated, along with your other expenses.

A vacation home is generally considered a residence if you use it for personal purposes for more than the greater of 14 days per year or 10 percent of the number of days the home is rented out at a fair rental value. Personal use is use by you or a co-owner of the property, or a family member of either, and use by other people who do not pay a fair market rental. Days when you are performing maintenance and repairs on a vacation property are not considered personal-use days. If you own a vacation home and rent it out to others, the amount of rental activity will affect the tax treatment of rental income:

- More than 14 days personal use/rented fewer than 15 days. If you rent out a home for 14 days per year or less, it qualifies as a second residence. Any rental income is tax-free, and any rental expenses are not deductible (except mortgage interest and real estate taxes).

- More than 14 days personal use/rented more than 14 days. If you rent out your vacation home for more than 14 days per year, and your personal use exceeds the greater of 14 days or 10 percent of the rental period, the home is a personal residence subject to the vacation home rules. You can deduct a proportionate share of property taxes and interest attributable to your personal use. The balance of the interest and taxes can reduce the rental income. In addition, you can deduct depreciation and other operating expenses attributable to the rental to the extent of any remaining rental income. Note that you cannot deduct expenses *in excess* of the rental income.

- Fewer than 15 days personal use/rented more than 14 days. If you rent your home for more than 14 days and your personal use does not exceed the greater of 14 days or 10 percent of the rental period, the vacation home is considered a rental property. Interest and taxes are allocated between personal and rental use of the property. In addition, other expenses allocable to the rental activity can be considered in full, even if this results in a loss. The loss, however, will be subject to the passive activity rules discussed next (also see Chapter 2) and generally will be deductible only to the extent of passive activity income. Interest allocated to your personal use of the home is personal interest and may not be deductible because the home generally is not considered a residence.

Rental Properties

If your vacation home is fully rented without any personal use, it is considered a rental property and is not subject to the special vacation home rules. As a rental property, taxes, interest, and other expenses are deductible, subject to the passive activity loss rules. Up to $25,000 of passive rental real estate losses can be deducted each year against other income such as compensation and interest, if the owner meets certain "active participation" requirements.

However, the $25,000 exception is decreased for homeowners with an AGI over $100,000 and is fully phased out for homeowners with an AGI over $150,000. Passive activity losses that can't be used currently are carried forward and can be deducted against future passive activity income, or are deducted in full when the activity that generated the losses ceases because of a disposition.

Home Office Deduction

Home is where the office is for a growing number of consultants, entrepreneurs, and telecommuters. Although expenses associated with use of a residence are generally not deductible, a home office deduction is permitted for certain expenses if a portion of the home is used exclusively and on a regular basis as the principal place of business or as a place to meet or deal with customers or clients in the ordinary course of the homeowner's trade or business.

In addition, home office deductions are available to homeowners who use a separate structure that is nearby, but not attached to the home, regularly and exclusively in connection with their trade or business.

Exclusive and Regular Use

To meet the exclusive-use requirement, you as the homeowner must use a portion of the residence solely for conducting business. There is no provision for *de minimis* personal use, such as typing a personal letter or making a personal phone call. If you are employed by a company, your use of the home office also must be "for the convenience of the employer." Generally, if your employer supplies you with an office, your home office use wouldn't meet this test.

Principal Place of Business

Until a few years ago, "principal place of business" was defined very restrictively for purposes of the home office deduction, preventing many who worked from their homes from claiming deductions.

However, a tax law change that went into effect in 1999 opened up the deduction to many more home office users. In addition to the place where the central functions of a business are performed, the term "principal place of business" now includes areas used for a business' administrative or management activities, if there is no other fixed location where the homeowner conducts these activities. This is the case even if most of the other work of the business is done outside of the home office. So, for example, it will be easier for salespeople, tradespeople, and manufacturers' representatives who work out of their homes, but perform much of their work at their customers' locations, to claim home office deductions. Here again, if you are an employee, use of your home must be for your employer's convenience to claim a home office deduction.

More people who work at home are able to take a home office deduction. Typical expenses include a portion of rent, depreciation, repairs, and utilities.

> ### Observation
> Under this liberalized definition of principal place of business, more individuals also are able to deduct the cost of traveling to and from their home (as their principal place of business) to other business locations. In the past, these transportation costs were considered nondeductible commuting expenses.

> **Observation**
>
> The rules about home office deductions are still complex. A separate tax form is required with Form 1040 to claim the deduction. (Self-employed individuals claim home office expenses on Form 8829 and on Schedule C; employees use Form 2106 or Form 2106EZ and claim them as miscellaneous itemized deductions on Schedule A Form 1040, subject to 2 percent of the AGI floor.)

Another consideration in evaluating whether it makes sense to take the deductions is that the portion of the home for which home office deductions are claimed may not qualify for the home sale exclusion described later in this chapter.

Personal Residence Trust

A first or second home is an ideal asset to transfer to a personal residence trust—a popular gift tax planning technique (see Chapter 7). In this case, the property is transferred to the trust for a period of years, during which you retain the right to live in or use the property. At the end of the term, the property passes to whomever you choose, either in further trust or outright. The value of the transfer is discounted for gift tax purposes because of your retained right to live in the residence. In addition, all future appreciation in the value of the home is transferred free of gift tax.

Although your beneficiaries will own the residence (either in trust or outright) at the end of the trust term, you can lease the property from them at a fair rental value. If you die before the end of the trust term, the property remains in your estate. Consequently, the retained right to live in the property or to use it should be for a reasonable period given your age and general health.

> ### Observation
>
> The personal residence trust's governing instrument (the document that creates the rules of the trust) must prohibit the trust from selling or transferring the residence, directly or indirectly, to you, your spouse, or an entity controlled by you or your spouse, during the time in which the trust is a grantor trust (a trust in which the grantor keeps some interests and control and therefore is taxed on any income from the trust). This means that the grantors will not be able to get the income tax basis step-up at death if they live beyond the trust term. This makes a personal residence trust less attractive for homes that are already highly appreciated.

Home Sales

Principal Residence Gains Exclusion

As a home seller, you may exclude up to $250,000 of gain from the sale of your home as long as it is owned and used by you as your principal residence for at least two of the five years before the sale. Qualifying married taxpayers filing jointly may exclude up to $500,000. The full exclusion is not available if, within the two-year period before the sale, you sold another home for which you claimed the exclusion.

Qualifying for the $500,000 Exclusion

A married couple filing jointly may exclude up to $500,000 of gain from the sale of their home if:

- Either spouse owned the home for at least two of the five years preceding the sale.
- Both spouses used the home for at least two of the five years preceding the sale.

- Neither spouse sold another home at a gain within the previous two years and excluded all or part of that gain using the exclusion.

Those in the military on official extended duty (stationed at least 50 miles from home or required to live in government quarters) may elect to suspend the five-year period for up to 10 years.

Partial Exclusion

A partial exclusion may be available if you do not meet the two-year ownership and use requirement, or sell your home within two years of a previous home sale for which you used the exclusion. If you fail to meet either requirement because of a change in employment, health, or certain other unforeseen circumstances as determined by the IRS, including separation or divorce and multiple births arising from the same pregnancy, the exclusion is based on the ratio of qualifying months to 24 months (or, if less, on the ratio of the number of months between the sale date of a previous home for which the exclusion was claimed and the sale date of the current home to 24 months).

For example, suppose a single person owned and used a home as a principal residence for one year (and did not previously use the exclusion on another home sale within the previous two years) and must move for job-related reasons. The partial exclusion rule allows this person to exclude up to $125,000 of his or her gain from the sale of the residence ($250,000 exclusion times 12 divided by 24).

Partial Exclusion Rule for Joint Filers

If a married couple filing jointly doesn't meet all the conditions for claiming an exclusion of up to $500,000, the gain that is excluded on the home sale is the sum of the exclusion each spouse would be entitled to if both were single. For this purpose, each spouse is treated as owning the home for the period that either spouse owned the home.

For example, a couple sells a home that one spouse owned and used as a principal residence for 10 years and the other spouse used as a principal residence for only one year. They sell the home because of illness. They may exclude up to $375,000 of profit from the sale ($250,000 for one spouse, plus $125,000 for the other spouse).

Observation

Special care and planning is needed to preserve the full home sale exclusion in divorce situations.

Observation

Home sellers in hot, upscale real estate markets will have to pay capital gains tax on any profit above the $250,000/$500,000 limits. The rollover break that used to defer unlimited amounts of home sale gain, provided an equally expensive residence was purchased as a replacement, is no longer available. However, the 2003 Tax Act's reduced capital gains rates drop the tax on these gains from 20 percent to 15 percent for home sales after May 5, 2003. Since the new exclusion is available once every two years regardless of whether it has been used before, some homeowners may decide to sell before their gains exceed the limits. Then additional gain on their replacement residence could also qualify for the exclusion in another two years.

Observation

Because a vacation home is not your principal residence, it does not qualify for tax-free treatment when it is sold. A residence that you also use as a vacation home cannot be swapped tax-free for another property in a like-kind exchange.

Observation

However, a vacation home could become your principal residence, and, therefore, qualify for the home sale exclusion. For example, if you own a principal residence where you have resided for two or more years and a vacation home, you can sell your principal residence and get the benefit of the home sale exclusion. Then if you move into your vacation home and establish it as your principal residence for at least two years, you can get the home sale exclusion on its sale.

Home Purchases

Real Estate Taxes

In general, real estate taxes can be deducted. In the year of a home sale, however, the Tax Code requires the deduction for real estate taxes to be apportioned between the buyer and seller according to the number of days each held the property during the year. It does not matter that your sales contract contains a different division of responsibility for the taxes.

Observation

Even though the buyer or seller might pay the entire tax, the deduction is limited by the statutory formula.

Observation

You will need your closing statement from a home sale or purchase to calculate the amount of deductible real estate taxes. You will also need to know whether the states in which you purchased or sold a home require prepayment of real estate taxes or whether such taxes are paid in arrears.

Sales Tax

Since the 1986 Tax Act, sales tax paid on nonbusiness purchases has been a nondeductible expense. The 2004 Tax Act provides individuals with a year-by-year election to deduct sales tax instead of state and local income tax. This election is only available for tax years beginning after December 31, 2003, and before January 1, 2006 (the 2004 and 2005 calendar tax years). Thus, on a home purchased in 2005, sales tax on home furnishings may be large enough to exceed state and local income tax.

Mortgage Points

Mortgage points incurred with a home loan can be significant. A *point* is a charge paid by a borrower for taking out a loan. Each point is 1 percent of the loan amount. You must amortize most points over the life of the loan; however, you can deduct points you pay for acquiring or making improvements to your main residence in the year the points are paid. The deductibility of points depends on whether the lender assesses them as additional interest or as a service charge. This is sometimes a difficult determination. Points are generally considered additional interest if the lender is charging for the use of money. If points are assessed for application preparation or processing, they are treated as a service charge and added to the purchaser's basis in the residence and thus are nondeductible.

Observation

Do not assume you should pay points when purchasing a new home. Think about how long you are likely to own the property. If you expect to sell the property within five years or less, it may be more advantageous to pay a slightly higher interest rate to get a no-points or low-points mortgage loan.

Points may be deducted in full during the year they were paid if the following requirements are met:

- Points are paid directly to the lender by the borrower; points are treated as paid directly to the lender if the borrower provides un-borrowed funds at least equal to the points charged at the closing or as a down payment or escrow deposit.
- The loan is incurred for the purchase or improvement of a principal residence.
- Points are an established business practice in the area in which the loan originates. In other words, banks and other lending institutions in that geographical area typically impose points when granting mortgage loans.
- The dollar amount of the points is typical for the area in which the loan originates.
- The points are clearly designated as such on the settlement form.
- The points are expressed as a percentage of the loan amount.

Thus, points paid on most mortgage loans financing the purchase of principal residences are deductible. However, borrowers who do not satisfy these requirements must amortize the points over the life of the loan.

Observation

The most common situations in which points must be amortized include the purchase of a second residence and refinancing the mortgage on the principal residence.

Observation

The unamortized points remaining when an underlying mortgage is paid off after a sale or refinancing are deductible in full. But points on a satisfied mortgage cannot be deducted immediately on a refinancing if the same mortgage lender holds both mortgages.

Idea Checklist

☑ Convert nondeductible interest expense into tax-deductible home-equity interest expense.

☑ Know the vacation home rules before renting out your second home.

☑ Consider placing a principal residence or second home in a personal residence trust.

☑ Review closing documents from real estate sales or purchases to find deductible real estate tax amounts.

☑ If you refinance your home during 2005, any remaining un-amortized points on the paid-off loan are generally deductible on your 2005 return.

☑ Rather than paying tax on a large gain on a vacation home, consider converting it to your principal residence for two years before the sale in order to make up to $250,000/$500,000 of your gain tax-free.

Owning a home is a cornerstone of the American Dream, and a home has usually been most taxpayers' most valuable asset, both financially and emotionally. The tax law gives home ownership numerous opportunities that this chapter has described.

Chapter 5 discusses saving for education—a high priority under the 2001 Tax Act. In the past, many of the Tax Code's incentives for education savings were not available to taxpayers in the higher brackets. Now, however, families with relatively high incomes may be able to put away more after-tax money and withdraw the gains tax-free, which increases their flexibility for funding education for children and grandchildren. Chapter 5 looks at that in detail.

Chapter 5

HOW TO MAXIMIZE SAVINGS FOR EDUCATION

To pay for a child's quality education, parents will do just about anything, even spend their life savings, assume second mortgages, and work at multiple jobs if that's what's necessary. It gets harder and harder to keep up with college tuition that is growing far faster than the inflation rate.

Fortunately, the Tax Code now offers some real incentives to help parents fund their children's education. This chapter describes a number of helpful tuition-financing techniques. Despite the fact that there are more available tax breaks, the best advice is to put aside as much as you can as early as you can.

Until now, many of the education tax incentives weren't available to those with higher incomes. But families with higher incomes now can take advantage of some tax breaks, including what is by far the best educational tax break, the much-improved Section 529 plan. Also, many of the restrictions that previously prevented taxpayers from bundling various education tax breaks together in the same year have been eliminated.

> ### Observation
>
> Parents should consider the impact that Section 529 programs and Coverdell Education Savings Accounts (formerly called Education IRAs) will have on their chances of obtaining financial aid for college. Some advisors suggest that families who wish to maximize their financial aid use the types of investments that are favored in the federal financial aid formulas. These investments include retirement savings, life insurance, and home equity. However, there are many reasons not to engage in this type of planning:
>
> - The financial aid rules may change before your child is in college.
> - The favored assets under the federal formula may not be favored for your child's university-provided financial aid.
> - Most financial aid is in the form of loans, not grants—why burden yourself or your child with debt?
> - Only a small percentage of parental assets are applied to reduce each year's financial aid.

Qualified Section 529 Tuition Programs

For a number of years, the Tax Code has allowed states to set up "qualified state tuition programs," often referred to as Section 529 plans after the part of the Tax Code that authorizes them. States are permitted to offer two types of plans:

1. *Prepaid tuition plans* that allow a parent, grandparent, or other person to prepay tuition costs and certain other education expenses. Participants are generally allowed to put aside future tuition by contributing money to these plans, thus assuring tuition at today's tuition rate. These types of plans are generally

available only to state residents and are meant to be used for tuition at in-state public schools. About 20 states have these plans for their residents. Programs differ from state to state, however, and you have to look carefully at the details of your own state's plan.

2. *Tuition savings plans* that offer more flexibility on contribution limits and investment choices are not limited to use for attendance at in-state schools. They can be used to pay tuition, room and board charges, and other expenses required for enrollment at almost any higher education institution. These plans are available in all 50 states. They are treated as any other parental asset under federal financial aid guidelines. This means that only 5.5 percent of the plan assets are counted toward a family's expected contribution versus 35 percent of a student-held asset such as an education savings account or a custodial account. And now that higher education distributions from these plans are excluded from income, the distributions will not be included as student income in the financial aid formula used in determining the family's expected financial contribution to tuition and other expenses.

As good as Section 529 state tuition programs were in the past, they are now vastly better. Before 2002, earnings on prepaid amounts were tax-deferred until used to pay for the student's higher education. At that time, distributed earnings were taxable to the student beneficiary, who was usually in a lower tax bracket than the parent or other contributor. The educational fund built up faster, owing to tax deferral, and the tax that was ultimately owed was almost always much lower than it would have been at the parent-contributor's rate.

Now, however, distributions from these state tuition programs that are used to pay qualifying higher education expenses are completely tax-free until 2010. This applies to both prepaid tuition plans and tuition savings plans. As a result, they are a *much improved* higher education savings vehicle.

Legislative Alert

The Treasury Department has proposed that the exclusion for Section 529 plan distributions used to pay higher education expenses be made permanent.

Private educational institutions now are permitted to establish pre-paid tuition programs (but not tuition savings plans) that have the same tax benefits as state tuition plans.

Unlike most other tax-advantaged education savings vehicles, there are no limits to prevent high-income individuals from using Section 529 plans. Substantial sums can be accumulated for a beneficiary—more than $300,000 in some plans.

The private plans should be attractive to many parents and future students, especially families with a history of attendance at a particular private college. Currently there is one organization that has created a nationwide prepaid tuition program. The 529 plan permits the purchase of prepaid tuition that can be used at more than 200 private schools.

A rollover option allows transfers between the tuition plans of different states, between a state's prepaid tuition plan and its savings plan, or between a state tuition plan and a private plan. While the federal tax law permits rollovers, plans are not required to do so. If flexibility is important, make sure that the plan permits rollovers.

What Expenses Qualify?

Tax-free qualified tuition plan benefits (both state and private) are available to fund tuition, fees, books, and supplies. Most room and board expenses for students who attend school at least half time will also qualify. To figure the amount that can be received tax-free, expenses that would otherwise qualify must be reduced by tax-free scholarship grants, veterans' benefits, tax-free employer-paid educational expenses, and amounts that qualify for higher education tax credits. Also, amounts received tax-free from a qualified tuition plan reduce the amount of education expenses that qualify for the tuition deduction discussed on pages 119–120.

Distributions of earnings that exceed qualified expenditures are taxed to the beneficiary and are generally subject to a 10 percent excise tax. Amounts not used by the beneficiary can be rolled over to another beneficiary's account as long as the new beneficiary is a family member (including a spouse and even, a first cousin), thus keeping the tax benefits working for other family members. Earnings not used for qualified higher education expenses that are returned to the contributor are taxed at the contributor's rate plus the 10 percent excise tax. Earnings that are distributed because of the beneficiary's death or disability, or because of the beneficiary's receipt of a scholarship, are not subject to a penalty. Also not subject to the 10 percent excise tax are distributions of earnings that are taxable because the taxpayer elects to take the credits or deductions described in the prior paragraph.

Observation

The Tax Code imposes a 10 percent tax penalty for taxable distributions from Section 529 plans that are not used for education expenses. Before 2002, these plans had to impose a penalty on refunds not used for educational expenses. Some states have not removed their plan's penalty for nonqualified use of funds. However, this should not be a factor in choosing a state-qualified tuition plan as long as the plan permits rollovers. If there are funds in the account that will not be used for education expenses, the account could be rolled over and later distributed from a plan that does not impose a penalty of its own.

Legislative Alert

The Treasury Department has recommended that Congress create legislation that would:

- Require Section 529 plans to impose penalties on distributions in excess of $50,000 that are not used for qualified education expenses.

- Require distributions by the time the beneficiary reaches age 35.

- Prevent the custodian of the account from having a beneficial interest in the account.

- These rules would apply to accounts opened or contributed to after the date of enactment.

Contributions to qualified tuition plans may be made only in cash. Unlike Coverdell Education Savings Accounts, contributors and beneficiaries are not permitted to self-direct the investments in qualified tuition plans. However, most savings plans permit an initial investment selection among different investment types, and the account owner can switch investments once every 12 months and upon any change in account beneficiaries.

Many states also offer tax incentives to their residents, including state income tax deductions for some contributions to their state's qualified tuition plans. No state permits a deduction for contributions to a Section 529 plan sponsored by another state. Some states have changed or are considering changing the tax treatment of these programs to conform more closely to the federal tax exemption. Also, some states require a recapture of the state income tax deduction if funds are withdrawn and/or rolled over to another state's plan. The recapture is necessary to prevent the abuse of making contributions solely for the purpose of receiving state income tax deductions.

Caution

There are a number of special rules that coordinate the benefits of various tax-favored education savings vehicles. For example, if you take distributions in the same year from a Coverdell Education Savings Account and a qualified tuition program, and the cumulative distributions exceed the amount of higher education expenses that qualify for the tax breaks, the expenses must be allocated between the distributions to determine how much of each can be excluded. Also, you may claim a higher education tax credit—a HOPE or lifetime learning credit—if you otherwise qualify, and receive a tax-free distribution from a qualified tuition plan in the same year for the same student (but only to the extent that the distribution doesn't cover the same expenses for which the tax credit was claimed).

In addition to the tax advantages, Section 529 plans generally offer professional investment management. The plans of some states offer little flexibility in this regard; their investment choices are somewhat limited. In these plans, your funds usually are invested somewhat more aggressively when your child is younger and less so as the time horizon to begin paying for college nears. Other plans allow you to choose among various types of funds. However, don't expect to be able to time the market too closely. Federal tax law allows investment changes within a plan to be made no more than once a year. Since you are not limited to using your own state's plan, you can shop around and find one that gives you the kinds of investment management and choice that suits you. However, keep in mind that state tax deductions for contributions are available only to state residents who invest in their own state's Section 529 plan. To learn the details of these programs offered by the various states, log on to www.collegesavings.org/locator/index.htm or www.savingforcollege.com and click on your state.

Another thing to keep in mind is that anyone can set up a Section 529 plan. You do not have to be a parent. You can set one up naming a grandchild, nephew, or niece, or even an unrelated individual as beneficiary. Some plans permit you to be both the owner and the beneficiary. If you later want to change the beneficiary without incurring income tax, you can name another family member of the original beneficiary as the new beneficiary. You will need to supply the beneficiary's Social Security number, but there is generally no reason that the beneficiary would have to be informed of the plan's existence. With the exception of a few prepaid tuition plans, the beneficiary has no rights of any kind regarding a Section 529 plan. Therefore, the account owner must carefully consider who will become the successor owner upon the original account owner's death. The successor owner could choose to direct the money away from the intended beneficiary.

Gift and Estate Tax Breaks

Payments made into qualified tuition programs are considered completed gifts at the time payment is made into the program, even though the student-beneficiary may not receive the benefit of the gift for many years, and even though you retain control over the account. As a result, the payments are eligible for the $12,000 annual gift tax exclusion in 2006. In fact, five years' worth of annual-exclusion gifts can be made in one year to a qualified tuition plan. As a result, a married couple could give $60,000 each to the plan of the same beneficiary in a single year. However, no additional gifts from the couple could then be made to that beneficiary for the next four years without being subject to gift tax filings (see Chapter 7 for details). Furthermore, contributions and earnings in Section 529 plans generally won't be included in your taxable estate. Because of this, your education funding can do double duty as part of your estate plan.

Coverdell Education Savings Accounts

Coverdell Education Savings Accounts (formerly called Education IRAs) allows individuals to contribute up to $2,000 per year for a child to save for education. To make a full contribution, contributors cannot have AGI above $190,000 on a joint return or $95,000 if single. The contribution phases out for AGI between $190,000 and $220,000 on a joint return ($95,000 to $110,000 for singles).

Tax-free Coverdell Education Savings Account distributions can be used for kindergarten, primary-school, and secondary-school tuition and expenses as well as for higher education expenses. Qualified expenses include not only tuition and fees but also tutoring costs, room and board, uniforms, transportation, and extended-day programs. Even some computer equipment and Internet access qualifies if used by the beneficiary and the beneficiary's family during a year that the beneficiary is enrolled in school.

Any unused amounts in a Coverdell Education Savings Account must be distributed before the beneficiary turns 30 or be rolled over into a Coverdell Education Savings Account for another family member under age 30. Undistributed amounts are taxed to the beneficiary at that time. Eligible family members include the beneficiary's spouse, children, brothers and sisters, and nieces and nephews. If a distribution is not used for educational expenses, the beneficiary is taxed on the earnings and must pay a 10 percent penalty.

The HOPE Scholarship or Lifetime Learning Credits are available in the same year in which an income exclusion is claimed for distributions from a Coverdell Education Savings Account as long as expenses for which a credit is claimed aren't the same ones for which the exclusion is claimed.

Observation

Your children and grandchildren may be able to benefit from a Coverdell Education Savings Account even if your income exceeds the AGI threshold. Anyone can contribute to a Coverdell Education Savings Account for your child or grandchild.

(continued)

Continued

Grandparents, aunts, uncles, or even siblings can make the contributions, provided their income is below the modified AGI limitation. Even a child may contribute to his or her own Coverdell Education Savings Account. Also, companies now may make contributions to Coverdell Education Savings Accounts. If a parent's income is too high to make a contribution, his or her company may make the contribution to the child's Coverdell Education Savings Account. (Such a payment would be taxable compensation to the parent, the same as if the company paid the parent who, in turn, made the contribution to the account.)

Legislative Alert

The Treasury Department has recommended that Congress eliminate the income restrictions for Coverdell Education Savings Accounts.

Observation

Parents who intend to send their children to private elementary and secondary schools may want to use Coverdell Education Savings Accounts to help pay those costs and use qualified tuition programs to build a higher education fund. Contributions to a Coverdell Education Savings Account can be made until April 15 following the end of a year to which the contribution relates.

Impact of Lower Capital Gains and Dividends Taxes

The reduced tax rate on qualified dividends and capital gains (see Chapters 1 and 2) should have little impact on the decision to participate in state sponsored college savings programs (Section 529 plans) or Coverdell Education Savings Accounts. These plans offer the potential for tax-free appreciation on stocks (dividend paying or otherwise) as long as funds are used for education.

Roth IRAs

Roth IRAs have a special distribution payout rule that makes them a good source of tax-advantaged cash for education funding. If you withdraw funds from a regular IRA to pay for college while you are under age 59½, the withdrawal is mostly, if not completely, taxable. With a Roth IRA, however, you can withdraw up to the amount of your contributions tax-free for any purpose, even if you are under age 59½. Earnings on the contributions are deemed withdrawn only after you have withdrawn *all* contributions. If you need to withdraw earnings on the contributions to pay for qualified education expenses, they will be included in your gross income but will not be subject to the usual 10 percent early withdrawal penalty.

Example

John Smith contributes $3,000 a year to a Roth IRA for 10 years. At the end of that period, he can withdraw his $30,000 cumulative contribution both income tax and penalty free. Earnings on the contributions remain in the account to further compound for his retirement.

Observation

The increased IRA contribution limits that have begun to be phased in (see Chapter 3 for details) make this strategy even more useful.

Traditional IRAs

Traditional IRAs are generally not as good a source for funding education expenses as the other vehicles described in this chapter because all distributions are included in income if all contributions were deductible. (If nondeductible contributions were made, part of each distribution is taxable and part is considered to be a return of capital.) However, if an IRA withdrawal is used to pay for qualified educational expenses for you or your spouse, child, or grandchild, no 10 percent early withdrawal penalty is imposed. Qualified educational expenses include tuition, fees, books, supplies, and required equipment at a postsecondary school.

> ### Observation
> This penalty exception for higher education expenses does not apply to premature distributions from qualified retirement plans, but it does apply to simplified employee pension (SEP) plan distributions, which are treated as IRAs for this purpose.

HOPE Scholarship and Lifetime Learning Credits

Taxpayers may be eligible to claim a nonrefundable HOPE Scholarship tax credit or a Lifetime Learning tax credit against their federal income taxes for qualified tuition and related expenses.

A HOPE Scholarship tax credit provides up to $1,500 in tax credits per student, but only for each of the first two years of at least half-time college enrollment. A Lifetime Learning tax credit is also available, now providing an annual 20 percent tax credit on the first $10,000 of tuition and related expenses, for a maximum of $2,000 per year. The Lifetime Learning credit maximum applies per-household, not per student, and can be claimed for yourself, your spouse, or your child. Note that only one of these credits can be claimed in any year for the expenses of a given student.

Students claimed as dependents may not take either credit on their own tax returns. Qualifying educational expenses that a dependent student pays are treated as paid by the person who claims the student as a dependent for purposes of figuring that person's HOPE credit. Amounts paid to educational institutions by third parties, such as grandparents, are treated as paid by the student (and, in turn, by the student's parents if they claim the student as a dependent).

If you are above the income threshold in 2005 for these credits (availability of the credits phases out between a modified AGI of $43,000 and $53,000 for singles; $87,000 and $107,000 for married couples filing jointly), there may still be some opportunities to benefit from the credits. If you forgo claiming your student-child as a dependent, and the child has sufficient taxable income to be able to use the credit, the tax value of the credit may be more than you lose by giving up the dependency exemption. There is no restriction on the type of income that may be offset by the tax credit, so a child's investment income would qualify.

Observation

The higher your income, the better this trade-off is, since your ability to claim dependency deductions on a 2005 joint return starts to phase out at $218,950 of adjusted gross income and disappears completely above $341,450.

U.S. Savings Bonds

You may exclude from income any interest received on redemption of U.S. savings bonds purchased after 1989 when you are 24 or older if qualifying educational expenses for the tax year exceed the aggregate proceeds received from redemption of bonds.

Observation

The ability to use this provision in 2005 begins to phase out for single individuals with an AGI of $61,200 and married couples with an AGI of $91,850. The phase-out range for the interest exclusion is $15,000 for singles and $30,000 for joint-return filers. Because the income level is measured in the year the bonds are redeemed (which might be years into the future), you may not be able to take advantage of the provision if income levels are too high at that time. The interest income would then be subject to tax at ordinary rates.

If you are concerned that your income may be too high in the year of redemption, it might make more sense to invest in growth stocks. This will allow you to manage the capital gains income and you could transfer the stock to your child on a "just-in-time" basis, to be sold at reduced capital gains rates (see "Income Shifting and Capital Gains," page 120).

Example

Mr. Jones redeems series EE bonds in the amount of $20,000. Mr. Jones paid $12,000 for the bonds in 1991 and would have to recognize $8,000 of interest income upon the redemption. If Mr. Jones has qualifying education expenses of at least $20,000 during the tax year in which he redeems the bonds and his income is low enough, he avoids income tax on the interest income from the bond redemption. Qualifying educational expenses include tuition and fees spent for the taxpayer, the taxpayer's spouse, and dependents of the taxpayer.

Home-Equity Loans

If you need to borrow to pay college expenses, consider a home-equity loan. You can claim the loan interest as an itemized deduction, up to a maximum debt amount of $100,000. However, home-equity debt interest in this case would not be deductible for alternative minimum tax purposes.

Student Loans

You may deduct up to $2,500 of interest paid on qualified education loans (loans taken out and used solely to meet higher education expenses), which you are liable to repay, even if you don't itemize deductions. Interest on loans from relatives or other individuals can't be deducted.

The student-loan interest deduction phases out at a modified AGI level between $50,000 and $65,000 for singles, and $105,000 and $135,000 for married joint-return filers.

Observation

Due to the phase-out thresholds, many parents are shut out of this deduction because their family income is too high. If borrowing is necessary in these situations, it usually makes sense for the student rather than the parent to take out as much of the loan as possible to generate maximum tax benefits. The deduction is not available to a child for any year when the child is claimed as a dependent on the parents' tax return. However, the child is not likely to be a dependent when the loan is being repaid following graduation. At that time, parents can make gifts to the child to help with loan repayment.

Tuition Deduction

Through 2005 only, a limited amount of higher education expenses are deductible by itemizers and nonitemizers alike. As with most education tax breaks, those with higher incomes won't be able to claim this. A deduction of up to $4,000 is permitted in 2004 and 2005, for singles with an AGI no higher than $65,000 or married couples with income no higher than $130,000. A maximum $2,000 deduction is available for those with higher incomes of up to $80,000 for singles and $160,000 for married couples. The deduction isn't available to those who can be claimed as dependents on another person's tax return.

There are also other restrictions. The tuition deduction can't be claimed for a year if a HOPE or Lifetime Learning credit is claimed for the same student. Also, no deduction will be allowed for the part of a qualified tuition plan distribution, savings bond redemption, or Education Savings Account that represents tax-free earnings; however, the part of the distribution representing a return of capital does qualify for the deduction.

Legislative Alert

The deduction for higher education expenses and student loan interest would be replaced by a per-student, not per-household, lifetime learning credit with a higher income eligibility under a Treasury Department proposal.

Relatives

Relatives, especially grandparents, with taxable estates (those that exceed the $1.5 million estate allowance that applies in 2005 or $2 million in 2006) may be looking for methods to reduce their estates despite additional future increases in the amounts that may escape estate tax (see Chapter 7). Payments of tuition made directly to an educational institution do not count against the gift tax annual exclusion amount, as explained on page 143.

Income Shifting and Capital Gains

As discussed in Chapter 2, the new, lower capital gains tax rates make it worthwhile to consider shifting income to your children who may pay only a 5 percent tax on capital gains.

Observation

If you expect to have capital gains from selling stock to pay for college or another major expense for a child age 14 or older, consider giving the asset to the child, who can then sell it. Assuming that the child is in a 10 percent or 15 percent tax bracket, the child will pay tax at the 5 percent capital gains rate (even if the asset is sold the next day) as long as the combined holding period exceeds 12 months. Keep in mind that both your purchase price and date of purchase will transfer to gift recipients.

Observation

Remember, in 2006, the gift tax may apply to gifts over $12,000 from single individuals and $24,000 from married couples.

Observation

To fund college or other expenses for children, consider assets that are likely to provide superior capital appreciation over the minimum one-year-plus holding period. These assets can now be held in the child's name (in a Uniform Gifts to Minors Act [UGMA] or Uniform Transfers to Minors Act [UTMA] account) or in trust (as long as the trustee has the ability to distribute capital gains) or be a gift to the child on a "just-in-time" basis, since there would be a carryover purchase price and purchase date.

Observation

If qualifying for financial aid is a possibility, it may be wise to keep assets in the parents' names and transfer them to the student on a just-in-time basis. This is because the federal financial aid family contribution formula requires parents to contribute a smaller percentage of their assets than students must.

Employer Education Assistance

Many employers, especially larger ones, have benefit plans that provide up to $5,250 a year of education assistance to employees. This benefit is tax-free to employees if it applies to tuition and related expenses, such as fees, books, and certain associated supplies and equipment. Other related expenses, such as meals, lodging, and transportation, aren't covered by the income exclusion. The courses do not have to be job-related for the benefit to be tax-free. So, for example, a person who works as a clerk or secretary at a company could take courses toward a degree in literature, history, or economics and receive tax-free benefits. Tax-free assistance is not available, however, for courses involving sports, games, or hobbies.

An employee, whose employer's plan permits, can receive tax-free benefits to attend graduate school part-time while working. Tax-free benefits are not available to companies whose education assistance plan discriminates in favor of highly compensated employees and their dependents. However, union employees don't have to be covered if education assistance was the subject of good faith bargaining.

If your employer doesn't have an education assistance plan, but reimburses you for education expenses, the reimbursement is tax-free if the education is job-related, that is, if it maintains or improves a skill currently used in your trade or business or is required to continue your employment. However, the courses can't qualify you for a new profession (such as law school courses taken by a CPA or MBA) or be needed for you to meet the minimum educational requirements for your current position.

If you pay for job-related courses on your own, without being reimbursed by your employer, you can deduct the expenses on your own tax return as miscellaneous itemized deductions. However, you can only claim otherwise deductible miscellaneous expenses that exceed 2 percent of your adjusted gross income and these deductions aren't allowed for AMT.

Table 5.1   Tax Breaks for Education

Type of Arrangement	Main Features	Income Limits
Qualified tuition plans	Post-2001 (post-2003 for private plan) distributions for higher education expenses are tax-free. Large gift-tax-free contributions can be made. Can be transferred to other family members.	None
Coverdell Education Savings Accounts	Per-child contribution limit: $2,000. Tax-free distributions for education. Can be used for kindergarten through postgraduate, including school-related computer equipment purchase and room and board. Broad investment choice.	Contribution limit phases out between a modified AGI of $95,000–$110,000 for singles; $190,000–$220,000 for joint filers.
Education savings bond exclusion	Interest is tax-free on redemption for higher-education expenses (but not room and board). Proceeds can be transferred to Coverdell ESA or qualified tuition plan. Child can't own bonds.	Exclusion phases out for 2005 between a modified AGI of $61,200 and $76,200 for singles, or $91,850 and $121,850 for joint filers.
Student loan interest deduction	Up to $2,500 of student loan interest deductible, even by nonitemizers. Can't be claimed by tax dependent.	Maximum deduction phases out between a modified AGI for 2005 of $50,000–$65,000 for singles; $105,000–$135,000 for joint filers.

(continued)

Table 5.1 *(Continued)*

Type of Arrangement	Main Features	Income Limits
Tuition deduction	Maximum $4,000 deduction for 2005 only. Not available if higher education tax credit is claimed for the same student.	$4,000 deduction available for singles with a modified AGI of up to $65,000 ($130,000 for joint filers). $2,000 deduction available for singles with a modified AGI of $65,000–$80,000, and $130,000–$160,000 for joint filers.
Higher-education tax credits	HOPE credit: up to $1,500 per student for first and second year of post-secondary education. Lifetime Learning credit: per household—maximum $2,000.	Phases out between a modified AGI of $43,000–$53,000 for singles; $87,000–$107,000 for joint filers for 2005.
Roth IRA distributions for higher-education expenses	Tax-free after 59½ if plan established five years. Distributions tax-free and penalty-free up to amount of contributions. Exempt from premature distribution penalty, even if distribution is taxable.	None for favorable tax treatment of distributions.
Traditional IRA distributions for higher-education expenses	Taxable to same extent as other IRA distributions, but exempt from 10% premature distribution penalty.	None
Education-assistance plan	Up to $5,250 of employer-provided education assistance is tax-free. Does not have to be job-related education Includes graduate study.	None

Idea Checklist

☑ Fund a qualified Section 529 tuition plan, especially if your income exceeds the threshold for Education Savings Accounts.

☑ If you qualify, fund a Coverdell Education Savings Account and a qualified tuition plan if you plan to send your children to a private elementary or high school.

☑ Have lower-income family members establish Coverdell Education Savings Accounts for children and grandchildren; alternatively, have children contribute to their own Coverdell Education Savings Accounts.

☑ Shift capital gains income into a 5 percent bracket by giving stock to your children or grandchildren age 14 or older.

☑ If loans are needed to help pay for educational expenses, first consider a home-equity loan.

☑ Be sure relatives know that tuition can be paid directly to an educational institution in addition to annual exclusion gifts, and that up to five years' worth of annual exclusion gifts can be made at one time to a qualified Section 529 tuition program.

☑ Consider funding a Roth IRA so you can withdraw your contributions tax-free and penalty-free to pay for college.

☑ Be aware of the higher income thresholds for some education tax incentives to know if you qualify for any that you couldn't use in past years.

☑ Consider not claiming your child as a tax dependent if your child has enough income to benefit from a higher education tax credit.

☑ Determine whether the new lower capital gains and dividends tax rates make saving for higher education outside of special tax qualified vehicles a viable option, after taking account of financial aid implications.

The tax law makes paying for college much more affordable for many (see Table 5.1 on pp. 123–124). Parents need creative ways for turning tax burdens into tuition tamers, a need that Congress has begun responding to in the ways this chapter has described.

Higher education can be a large expense for a family. But medical expenses can also be very costly. Fortunately, the tax law now provides some ways in which to pay for medical expenses in a favorable way, as you will see in Chapter 6.

Chapter 6

ACCOUNT-BASED HEALTH CARE ARRANGEMENTS

The Medicare Prescription Drug, Improvement, and Modernization Act in 2003, designed primarily to create prescription drug programs for Medicare beneficiaries, also established Health Savings Accounts (HSAs), which provide individuals with a tax-advantaged vehicle for paying medical expenses. Moreover, over the past few years, the IRS has supported company plans to provide medical benefits to employees on a tax-advantaged basis by issuing a number of favorable rulings, including through the recognition of Health Reimbursement Arrangements (HRAs). HSAs and HRAs are in addition to Health Flexible Spending Accounts (health FSAs) that employers have traditionally made available to employees.

What Are Health Savings Accounts?

HSAs are tax-advantaged investment or retirement accounts that you can use to pay for qualified medical expenses. To be eligible to contribute to an HSA, you must be covered under a qualifying high deductible health plan (HDHP). You and/or your employer may contribute to the HSA up to a specific limit. You can make contributions and claim a tax deduction, or, if your employer allows, you can make pretax contributions through your employer's cafeteria plan. If your employer contributes to your HSA on your behalf, those contributions are not taxable to you (and are not subject to Social Security and Medicare taxes). Once money is in your HSA, it belongs to you. You own the account and can take it with you when you leave the company.

Funds in your HSA account build up on a tax-free basis and are carried forward year to year. You can withdraw money and use it tax-free to pay for qualified medical expenses that you, your spouse, or your dependents incur (including long-term care expenses and insurance). Withdrawals for any other purpose are taxable and, if you are under age 65, subject to a 10 percent penalty.*

Observation

Nobody monitors withdrawals from HSAs to see that they are used for medical purposes. It is your responsibility to keep receipts and other proof to show the IRS that you used withdrawals for a tax-free purpose.

Eligibility

Whether you are covered by an HDHP from your employer or by your own policy, make sure it meets the tax law requirements so you can contribute to an HSA. Premiums for an HDHP are lower than for traditional, more extensive medical insurance.

HSAs are open to anyone who, on the first day of the month, meets the following requirements:

• Is covered by a plan that meets the definition of a high-deductible health plan.

• Is not covered by another type of health coverage (other than certain specific types of coverage, such as workers' compensation,

---

* HSA Coalition (www.hsainsider.com).

long-term care, disability, vision, or insurance for specific illness or disease).

- Is not eligible for Medicare
- Cannot be claimed as a dependent on someone else's tax return.

For 2005, a high-deductible health plan is defined as a plan with an annual deductible of at least $1,000 for self-only coverage or $2,000 for family coverage and the sum of the annual deductible and other annual out-of-pocket expenses is no more than $5,100 for self-only or $10,200 for family coverage (these dollar limits are adjusted annually for inflation).

Contribution Limits

In general, you cannot make contributions that exceed your insurance plan's deductible. For 2005, contributions to your HSA by you and/or your employer are limited to $2,650 if you have self-only coverage or $5,250 if you have family coverage (i.e., any plan other than self-only); these limits are adjusted annually for inflation.

If you are age 55 or older by year-end, the contribution limit is increased by $600 in 2005 (increasing in $100 increments to $1,000 by 2009). Contributions are fully deductible as an adjustment to gross income; you do not have to itemize medical expenses to claim this deduction.

Like IRAs, you have until April 15, 2006, to make HSA contributions for 2005.

Health Reimbursement Accounts

HRAs generally are notional accounts to which your employer credits an amount on your behalf. Only your employer can contribute to an HRA—you cannot. You can draw from the account to pay qualified medical costs that you, your spouse, or your dependents incur that are not covered by insurance. You are not taxed on the contributions, or on the withdrawals.

Your employer may provide you with a credit or debit card to use in accessing funds in your account or require you to submit bills and receipts to obtain reimbursements. Your employer may allow you to carry over some or all of the funds in your HRA from year to year to increase your available funds in the following year. Most employers do not allow their employees to take their HRA balances with them when they terminate employment.

Flexible Spending Arrangements

Your company may allow you to contribute a portion of your compensation to a medical flexible spending arrangement (FSA). Your contributions are made on a pretax basis; you do not pay income tax on the salary reduction amounts you commit to the FSA.

You can access funds already contributed as well as funds you agree to contribute. For example, if you agree to $200 monthly salary reduction amounts for 2006, you can submit reimbursement for a $2,400 expense in January 2006 (even though you may only have actually contributed $200 to your FSA).

Funds in your FSA that are not used up by the end of the year are forfeited; you cannot carry them over to the next year or take a withdrawal for any other purpose.

Legislative Alert
Congress is considering a measure to allow a limited carryforward (say $500) of unused FSA contributions to the following year.

Funds in FSAs can be used for a wide range of qualified medical expenses, including over-the-counter nonprescription medications (e.g., antacids, allergy medications, cold remedies, pain remedies) taken to alleviate or treat a sickness or personal injury.

Observation

Withdrawals are not permitted for medications taken to maintain general good health, such as dietary supplements.

Chapter 7

ESTATE PLANNING IDEAS

The repeal of the federal death tax provides less relief from estate planning chores than most people expected. Loss of the income tax basis step-up could prove to be a nightmare. As detailed next and in Chapter 1, the federal estate tax rate began to phase down starting in 2002 and the estate tax will be completely repealed in 2010. The exemption amount increases during the transition period as the maximum rate of tax on estates and gifts decreases. The gift tax phases down, too, but it will not be repealed completely.

Offsetting those advantages somewhat in 2010, however, will be some generally unfavorable changes to the income tax rules for in-herited property, especially for those people with large estates. During the phase-down period, when the exemption amount reaches $3.5 million (in 2009), complications with preexisting estate plans could arise that could cause a surviving spouse to receive no prop-erty outright. Proper planning during this period may result in large tax savings for some. Another change has caused some states to add or increase their own death taxes, since they are losing revenue as a result of the repeal of the state death tax credit that previously off-set federal estate taxes. After 2010, the repeal of the estate tax is scheduled to "sunset," returning the estate and gift tax rules back to a 55 percent maximum tax rate and a $1 million exemption amount.

As was previously the case, estate and gift tax planning strategies can still protect significant amounts of property from being subject to transfer taxes. However, there is less certainty as to what the best solutions will be. This chapter focuses on important planning ideas to consider.

How the Estate and Gift Taxes Work

Estate and gift taxes currently work in tandem as a unified transfer tax system, with basically the same tax rates and similar exemption amounts applying to both taxes. It amounts to "pay me now or pay me later." However, as the amount exempt from estate tax has increased above $1 million (it is $1.5 million for 2005 and $2 million for 2006), the gift tax exemption amount is frozen at the $1 million level. In addition, the gift tax will continue, although at a reduced rate of 35 percent during 2010 when the estate tax is scheduled to be repealed.

Observation

If you previously used your full lifetime gift tax exemption when the maximum exemption amount was $675,000, you may think that you can make an additional $325,000 of tax-free gifts, in addition to your annual exclusion gifts, to reach the current maximum gift tax exemption amount of $1 million. That is not the case, however, due to the way prior gifts are figured when calculating the gift tax owed on current gifts. People who are already subject to the maximum 47 percent (for 2005) gift tax bracket (because of prior taxable gifts) can only make $266,489 of additional gifts before paying gift tax. This is because the increased exemption amount of $325,000 is implemented through an increase of $125,250 in the applicable credit amount. Thus, $125,250/.47 = $266,489.

Amounts Exempt from Tax

In 2005, you may transfer $11,000 ($22,000 for most married couples) to each of an unlimited number of individuals free of gift tax.

This limit increases to $12,000 in 2006 ($24,000 for married couples who elect gift splitting). To qualify for this annual gift tax exclusion, the recipient generally must have immediate access to the gift, although some gifts in trust can qualify, as can contributions to a qualified tuition program.

Unlimited amounts can be transferred directly to an educational institution or health-care provider free of gift tax to pay someone else's tuition or medical expenses.

Aside from the annual exclusion amount, there are even bigger breaks. You can transfer unlimited amounts to your spouse free of gift or estate tax by way of the unlimited marital deduction. In addition, you are able to transfer $1 million to children and others without paying any gift tax through the lifetime exemption. If you and your spouse agree to split your gifts, you can give a total of $2 million by using the lifetime exemptions of both spouses. Annual exclusion gifts, tuition, medical, and spousal transfers are in addition to, and do not count against, this exemption. (Special rules apply, however, if your spouse is not a U.S. citizen.) See Table 7.1.

Table 7.1 *Estate and Gift Tax Exemption Allowances*		
Year	**Estate Tax Exemption (in $ Millions)**	**Gift Tax Exemption (in $ Millions)**
2005	1.5	1
2006	2	1
2007	2	1
2008	2	1
2009	3.5	1
2010	N/A (tax repealed)	1
2011 and later	1	1

Starting in 2004, when the estate tax exemption increased to $1.5 million, the special deduction for qualified family-owned business interests was repealed.

Gift and Estate Tax Rates

After you have exceeded the exemption amount, the estate and gift tax rates outlined in Table 7.2 apply for 2005. Thus, the maximum estate and gift tax rate for 2005 is 47 percent. In future years, the maximum rates are as shown in Table 7.3.

Estate tax rates may be even higher than you think because lifetime taxable gifts are added to property owned at death for purposes of determining the applicable estate tax rate, although your estate receives a credit for gift taxes paid on the lifetime taxable gifts. Currently, the recipient of most property transferred at death receives an income tax basis equal to the fair market value of the property at the date of death. This means that income tax is avoided on the increase in the value of the property that occurred during the decedent's life, and the estate or heir can sell the asset immediately after the decedent's death and not pay any capital gains tax.

The rule is different for gifts made during life. Here, in computing the recipient's gain, the recipient receives your income tax basis in the gifted property. Thus, if he or she sells the gift property after re-

Table 7.2 *Estate and Gift Tax Rates*	
For Taxable Gifts and Estates Above ($)	**Rate (%)**
1,000,000	41
1,250,000	43
1,500,000	45
2,000,000	48

Table 7.3 *Maximum Estate and Gift Tax Rates*	
Year	**Highest Estate and Gift Tax Rates (%)**
2005	47
2006	46
2007	45
2008	45
2009	45
2010	35 (gift tax) 0 (estate tax)
2011 and later	55

ceipt, he or she pays capital gains tax on any appreciation that has occurred since you acquired it. On the plus side, the gift recipient gets to include your holding period in determining whether a sale by him or her qualifies for favorable long-term capital gains treatment.

With capital gains rates as low as 15 percent—and only 5 percent for those (such as children and grandchildren) who are in the 10 percent or 15 percent income tax brackets—it still may be worth considering whether lifetime giving makes sense in spite of the lack of income tax basis step-up for lifetime gifts. Be sure to consider both the income tax and the transfer tax consequences of your gifts.

In 2010, when the estate tax is scheduled to be repealed, the income tax basis step-up (basis increase to the property's value at the time of transfer) for assets received from a decedent will be limited. The heirs of decedents dying in 2010 will receive an income tax basis step-up that will eliminate capital gains tax on a total of no more than $1.3 million of gain that occurred during the decedent's life. Property inherited by a surviving spouse will generally get an additional $3 million of basis increase, allowing a total basis increase of no more than $4.3 million.

Observation

The dollar limits on basis step-up will not affect smaller estates. However, it will add income tax complications to estate planning considerations for those with larger estates.

Observation

Only property transferred outright to the surviving spouse or held in a special form of trust known as a qualified terminable interest property (QTIP) trust qualifies for the additional $3 million of income tax basis increase for property passing to surviving spouses. Many persons have estate plans in which bequests to surviving spouses are held in other forms of trusts that qualify for the marital deduction for estate tax purposes, but not for purposes of the $3 million basis increase—for example, general power of appointment trusts or estate trusts. Although these types of transfers may be adequate if death occurs before 2010, these trusts may not be sufficient if death occurs in 2010 because the opportunity to step up the basis by an additional $3 million would be lost.

Observation

In the past, estate plans often provided that retirement assets or other assets that may not be stepped up be left to the surviving spouse rather than children or other heirs. Under the post-2009 rules, the reverse may be desirable, since it may be necessary to use the maximum amount of step-up for post-2009 transfers to a surviving spouse. It is important to consider income tax consequences other than just the basis step-up, such as the option to make certain IRA withdrawal elections that are available only to the surviving spouse.

An estate's executor will choose which of a decedent's assets will receive the basis increase. Donors and executors will also be required to report information about certain transfers, including basis and holding period information, to the IRS and to donees and estate beneficiaries.

> ### Observation
>
> If some beneficiaries receive higher basis property, other beneficiaries may be burdened with higher capital gains on the sale of the property they inherit. Planning will be needed to make the most of available basis step-up and to keep the potential for family strife over this issue to a minimum.

> ### Observation
>
> For those interested in leaving assets to charity, retirement assets remain an excellent choice because retirement assets do not qualify for a step-up in basis either before or after the scheduled repeal of the estate tax.

Planning for Phase-Down and Repeal of the Estate Tax

What will all of these changes mean for you? They will mean more, rather than less, estate planning. First, you will have to make sure that during the transition period from now through 2009, when exemption amounts are increasing and the maximum tax rates are dropping, your existing will and your overall estate plan still do what you intended. If not, you will have to make adjustments.

Second, you will need to stay on top of future changes to the estate and gift tax rules. Most estate planning experts doubt that the new rules will be fully implemented because they are now scheduled to change. The House of Representatives has passed bills to make the estate tax repeal permanent, but the Senate hasn't shown a similar inclination, at least not in the current economic environment with budget deficits projected to increase further in coming years. As for complete repeal of the estate tax—even for one year—many professionals advise not to count on it. We cannot predict how the political or economic climate will change over the next five years—only time will tell.

Planning will be easiest for those whose estates fall below the increases in the exemption amounts through 2009, which would eliminate all federal estate tax liability. Many will not need more than simple wills, without even the usual credit shelter trusts, to avoid estate taxes during this time. However, if estates increase in size, or the estate tax returns to the 2001 rules after 2010, or they live in a state with an inheritance tax that is not tied to the federal exemptions, that won't be true. New plans that are more complicated will again be necessary.

During the phase-out period, flexibility will be needed. Some estate planners have suggested increasing the use of disclaimers (an election to decline the receipt of inherited property) to give surviving spouses the ability to balance estate tax savings with other financial needs. Wills may benefit from contingency language that would cause alternative provisions to kick in if the expected estate tax changes, repeal, and/or reinstatement do not occur as scheduled.

There are many tax-saving ideas you can use to reduce your estate. They are particularly helpful to high-net-worth individuals. One quick way to figure out whether you need estate tax planning is to look at your net worth (the value of the assets you own minus the liabilities you owe). Be sure to include the face value of the life insurance on your life that you own. If the total exceeds the exemption amount, you need to think about some planning ideas.

The sooner you act, the better because a gift made now removes future appreciation from your estate.

Example

Take the case of an individual who used his exemption to make a $600,000 gift in 1987, when that was the maximum exemption amount. He died in 2005 when the gift's value had grown to $2.5 million. Thus, he effectively removed $2.5 million from his estate by acting early. In addition, the first $900,000 of his estate is sheltered by his remaining exemption allowance ($1.5 million allowance for 2005 less $600,000 used in 1987). Had he not made the gift, his gross estate for tax purposes would have increased by $1.9 million.

Observation

Those with large estates should consider maximizing the early giving strategy using the $1 million gift tax exemption.

Draft a Will

Many people do not have a will. As a result, their state of residence generally will determine who receives their property at death and how and when the property is received. If you are married with children, in most states not having a will means your surviving spouse will not receive all your assets. In addition, you will miss the opportunity to generate some significant estate tax savings for your family.

Even if your estate is less than the estate and gift tax exemption allowance, you need a will to name a guardian for your minor children.

Review How Your Property Is Owned

Unless you live in a community property state (Arizona, California, Idaho, Louisiana, Nevada, New Mexico, Texas, Washington, Wisconsin, and, under certain circumstances, Alaska), in which all property acquired during marriage is treated as half-owned by each spouse, it is important for a married couple to consider how their property is owned.

For married couples, joint ownership with right of survivorship can be the ruin of an otherwise excellent estate plan, because the surviving spouse will automatically receive the property at the death of the first spouse. You may want it to go to your children or someone else. Although no estate tax will be paid because of the unlimited marital deduction, there might not be enough property to fund other estate planning options, such as the credit shelter trust.

An asset ownership review can also help determine whether gifts or property transfers should occur during life between spouses to make sure that each spouse has sufficient property in his or her name alone to help fund a credit shelter or family trust without regard to the order in which the spouses die.

Observation

A review of your assets will be more crucial than ever as exemption amounts increase over the next several years.

Consider State Death Taxes

The state death tax credit allowable against the federal estate tax is repealed for those dying in 2005 and it is replaced by a deduction for any taxes actually paid to any state on a decedent's gross estate.

Observation

Almost all states had a state death tax equal to the amount allowed as a federal credit. This generated tax revenues for the states without actually increasing the total amount of total estate tax due by decedents' estates. The state death tax credit is

an important source of revenue for many states. Many states
have decoupled their death tax from the state death tax credit
to replace the revenue lost by repeal of the credit. This issue is
continuing to evolve, and ultimately could influence the state
in which you choose to reside prior to your death.

Observation

A review of your assets will be more crucial than ever as exemption amounts increase over the next several years.

Give Gifts

Over time, a gift-giving program can remove hundreds of thousands
of dollars from your estate on a tax-free basis. Beginning in 2006,
you can give up to $12,000 ($24,000 if your spouse joins in the gift)
to each of any number of people each year, and you will not have to
pay gift tax. These amounts will be increased for future inflation.
Making these *annual exclusion* gifts removes property from your estate at no gift or estate tax cost, often shifting income-earning property to family members in lower income tax brackets. You also
remove future appreciation in the value of the gift property from
your estate.

In addition, there is an unlimited exclusion for any tuition you pay
directly to a school or medical care payments you pay directly to a
health-care provider on someone else's behalf. These tuition and
medical payments are gift tax-free, and they don't count toward the
annual gift tax exclusion. Even multiyear advance tuition payments
may be structured to be gift tax-free. Thus, a grandparent can pay
tuition directly to a school on behalf of a grandchild, pay health insurance premiums, and the orthodontist for the grandchild's braces,

and still give the grandchild $12,000 in 2006 without using up any of the lifetime exemption amount.

> ### Observation
>
> Tuition payments for a private elementary school, secondary school, or college all qualify for the unlimited gift tax exclusion, as long as a charitable contribution to the school would generate a charitable contribution deduction. Room and board, books, and similar expenses *do not* qualify for the tuition exclusion.

It should be noted that payments by parents and grandparents to a qualified tuition program do not qualify for the unlimited tuition gift tax break. Payments by parents and grandparents to these tax-favored college savings programs do count toward the annual gift tax exclusion limit. However, you can choose to treat a contribution for a beneficiary in 2006 that is over $12,000 as made equally over five years (the current year plus four more years). Thus, a $60,000 gift to a qualified tuition program for a single beneficiary in a single year can be gift tax-free. For the next four years, though, you couldn't give the beneficiary any additional annual exclusion gifts.

> ### Observation
>
> It's generally better not to wait until late in the year to make gifts. Instead, it is a good idea to get in the habit of making gifts in January each year. In a good year, an asset that is worth $12,000 in January could be worth significantly more by the end of December. By giving early, the post-gift appreciation also escapes gift tax. Even though this strategy might not have worked well during recent down years for stocks, its prudence has been proven over the years. There have been vastly more up than down stock markets over the years.

Observation

The reduction to 5 percent in the tax rate on dividends and capital gains for taxpayers in the 10 percent or 15 percent tax brackets increases the benefit to a parent (who is in a high income tax bracket) of making a gift of appreciated or dividend producing property to a child over 13 years of age (who is in one of the two lowest income tax brackets). In addition to the gift and estate tax benefits associated with such a gift, the family may realize an additional benefit of reducing—from 15 percent in the parent's hands to 5 percent in the child's hands—the income tax imposed on future dividends and capital gains generated by the gifted property.

Valuation Discounts

Transfers of certain types of assets, typically a minority interest in a business enterprise, may permit the use of a valuation discount for gift and estate tax purposes (so that the value for transfer tax purposes is below the value that might result from a sale of the enterprise). The value of the underlying property does not change, but how the property is owned may generate valuation discounts.

Example

The true fair market value of Asset A is $100. Asset A, for valid business reasons, is placed into a vehicle that is friendly to valuation discounts, such as a limited partnership. When all the limited partnership interests are given to children, the value reported on the gift tax return might be only $75, reflecting a 25 percent discount from the underlying fair market value because of the minority interest and lack of marketability of the limited partnership interests. Limited partnership and limited liability companies offer many nontax advantages, including retention of control for the donor and some protection from creditors of the donee.

Observation

The IRS has challenged valuation discounts taken when family limited partnership interests are given away in "deathbed" transfers—those made very close to the time of an individual's death. Also, you must disclose claimed valuation discounts on your gift tax return or lose the benefit of a statute of limitations that ends the IRS's ability to adjust the value of the gift.

If you own a majority interest in a business, you can make gifts of nonvoting shares or less than controlling amounts of voting shares that would be entitled to a minority discount that would be unavailable if they were transferred at your death. Such gifts would not receive an income tax basis step-up at your death, but future appreciation would be out of your estate. If your lifetime gifts of voting shares brought your voting rights below 50 percent, then all of your shares would be entitled to a minority discount at your death.

Caution

If at your death you own a limited partnership, limited liability company, or nonvoting shares while still controlling the entity, you will not get a minority discount on any of the interests you own.

Consider Trusts

Credit Shelter or Family Trust

Married couples should have this one basic trust if their combined assets exceed the estate and gift tax exemption allowance amount $1.5 million for 2005. Failure to have this trust can cost your family hundreds of thousands of dollars in estate taxes that could have been avoided.

Spouses with very large estates still need fully funded credit shelter trusts. However, the increases in estate tax exemption amounts will require those with relatively modest estates to reexamine the impact of credit shelter trusts. These provisions ensure that both spouses' estates get the full estate tax exemption. Their purpose is to leave trusts for children or other heirs with the maximum that can pass to them without estate tax, and to give surviving spouses only a limited interest in that portion of a decedent's estate. These provisions were designed around exemption amounts ranging from $600,000 to $1 million. As the exemption increases under the 2001 Act, however, these trust arrangements will be funded with larger and larger amounts—and possibly all— of a decedent's assets, in some cases leaving nothing outright to the surviving spouse. If the surviving spouse has sufficient assets and maximizing estate tax savings is the prime consideration, it may be a desirable outcome. In other situations, use of the credit shelter trust could cause serious financial problems for the surviving spouse.

Observation

Many wills now automatically increase the credit shelter trust's funding as the exemption amount rises. You can avoid this by specifying in your will the maximum amount of your estate that should fund a credit shelter trust, or the minimum amount that should be available to the surviving spouse.

Life Insurance Trust

If you have a life insurance policy, consider giving the policy to a life insurance trust or having the trust purchase a new policy directly from the life insurance company. If done properly, the policy proceeds can escape estate tax.

> ### Observation
>
> Life insurance needs for estate liquidity may decrease as the estate tax is phased out and repealed, but the need will not be eliminated because of the loss of full basis step-up and the possibility of reinstatement of the estate tax in 2011. You will have to take a variety of contingencies into account in drafting and funding a life insurance trust, particularly the anticipated need by your survivors for quick access to cash.

Grantor Retained Annuity Trust

This trust arrangement should be referred to as the "no downside trust." This trust is popular because it permits you to give away future appreciation on property in the trust while retaining the property's initial value plus a fixed return. The fixed return is legislatively provided and it is prescribed over the entire life of the arrangement based on the prevailing interest rate in the month the arrangement begins. If the trust assets provide a rate of return that exceeds the benchmark rate of return, the trust's beneficiaries can receive the excess (either in further trust or outright) at little or no gift tax cost.

Typical assets placed in this type of trust include S corporation stock, publicly traded stock, and other assets that are expected to grow quickly. The higher the rate of return, the greater the amount that will go to the trust's beneficiaries.

> ### Observation
>
> Gifts to these trusts are particularly attractive in periods of low interest rates (such as we are experiencing) because it should

be easier to exceed the benchmark rate of return. (The benchmark rate of return varies from month to month based on interest rates on U.S. Treasury securities.)

Qualified Personal Residence Trust

You can transfer a personal residence (either a principal residence or vacation home) to the beneficiaries of a qualified personal residence trust at a discount from the home's current fair market value. You can live in the home for a term of years and continue to take a mortgage interest deduction as well as a real estate tax deduction. When your term interest in the trust ends, you can rent the home from the trust or its beneficiaries at fair market value rates (an excellent means of further reducing your estate).

A qualified personal residence trust is especially desirable if significant appreciation is expected in the value of the home over time, because the appreciation that occurs after the trust is established can also escape estate and gift taxation.

Observation
Unlike grantor retained annuity trusts, gifts to these trusts are less attractive in periods of low interest rates because the gift tax cost is higher than it would be in periods of higher interest rates.

Dynasty Trust

A dynasty trust allows you to provide for your descendants (usually your grandchildren and more remote descendants) without gift, estate, or generation-skipping transfer tax consequences to your descendants. Such trusts are typically designed to last for the longest possible period allowed by law. Typically, the trustee (the individual or entity who manages the trust assets and income) will have the discretion to pay trust income and principal to your descendants. The trusts are intended to take advantage of some part or the entire amount that you can transfer to your grandchildren or more remote descendants without incurring the generation-skipping transfer tax. This amount for 2005 through 2009 is equal to the estate tax exemption amount as shown in Table 7.1 on page 135. A dynasty trust can be established during life or in a will.

Charitable Remainder Trust

If you are concerned because you have built up an asset base that is not producing sufficient cash flow for you, this trust may help. The rate of return is flexible—the cash-flow yield can be improved to 5 percent or higher on the value of your asset base. At the end of the term of the trust (which could be your lifetime), the remaining trust principal will pass to charity. Because these trusts are tax-exempt entities, they generally don't pay income tax upon the sale of any low-basis assets used to fund the trust, as you would have to if you sold the assets yourself to reinvest the proceeds. Thus, the trust will have more post-sale proceeds to reinvest than you would have to reinvest. Also, you will receive an income tax deduction for a portion of the initial value of the trust.

Observation

You can use some of the extra cash flow that you receive from this asset transfer and establish a life insurance trust for your family to replace the assets placed in the charitable remainder trust, which go to charity at your death. However, life insurance is not a required adjunct to a charitable remainder trust.

> **Observation**
> The income tax rate reductions and its decrease in the income tax rates imposed on dividends and capital gains diminish the tax benefits of charitable remainder trusts, making them relatively less attractive than they had been in the past.

Charitable Lead Trust

A charitable lead trust (CLT) provides that the charity receives an income stream for a period of years and the remainder goes to a family member or other noncharitable beneficiary. A charitable lead trust is the opposite of a charitable remainder trust (discussed earlier). There are two types of charitable lead trusts: the charitable lead annuity trust (CLAT) and the charitable lead unitrust (CLUT).

Upon creation of a CLT, the donor is entitled to an income tax charitable deduction if the charitable interest is in the form of a fixed percentage of trust assets or a guaranteed annuity *and* if the donor is taxed on the trust's annual income (i.e., a grantor trust). The tax liability can be mitigated if the trustee invests in tax-exempt securities. If the donor establishes a *nongrantor* charitable lead trust, he or she will not receive a charitable income tax deduction, but will not be taxed on the trust's income each year either.

Individuals who are charitably inclined can achieve important gift tax and estate planning objectives through the use of a charitable lead trust. In return for promising to make a certain level of charitable contributions, it can be possible for an individual to transfer the property remaining in the trust at some future date, without any gift or estate tax. The CLT is particularly beneficial in the low interest rate environment that we have been experiencing during the past several years.

> **Observation**
>
> Charitable lead trusts generally benefit from income tax reductions in the same ways that would result if the grantor held the CLT assets directly. However, there are factors that may make nongrantor CLTs less beneficial. Generally, a nongrantor CLT is entitled to an income tax deduction for the annuity amount that it pays to charity. This deduction is available only to offset CLT income. Therefore, the income tax deduction may reduce the benefit of a CLT because the value of the charitable deduction is reduced. There also may be factors that make nongrantor CLTs more beneficial. A CLT's charitable deduction is not subject to adjusted gross income limitations, or the 3 percent haircut on itemized deductions.

Intentionally Defective Trust

Transfers into this kind of trust are gifts, but the person making the gift is still liable for the tax on income earned by the trust. What is the benefit? The payment of the income tax provides an indirect advantage to the trust beneficiaries, since what they receive from the trust won't be diminished by income taxes owed by the trust, yet the grantor's payment of the income tax is not considered a further gift to the trust. The "defective" aspect refers to the fact that the person setting up the trust is liable for income taxes. At one time, when income tax rates were as high as 90 percent, that was considered bad. But for high-net-worth individuals, a defective trust can save a family a significant amount of estate taxes. Further tax savings may be obtained by selling property to the trust for a promissory note. If properly structured, the growth in the trust assets above the interest rate on the note may pass to your heirs free of gift or estate taxes.

Qualified Domestic Trust

A qualified domestic trust (QDOT) is a special trust that qualifies for the estate tax marital deduction even though the surviving spouse is not a U.S. citizen. Generally, the estate tax is deferred until the death of the surviving spouse, at which time an estate tax must be paid based on the value of the trust principal remaining. If distributions of trust principal are paid out to the surviving spouse before death, estate tax is also generally payable based on the value of that distribution. The QDOT principal will escape estate taxation at death if the surviving spouse dies in 2010 or thereafter. Also, any distributions of principal from a QDOT to a living spouse would remain subject to the estate tax through 2020 but would be free of estate tax in 2021. (Because 2021 occurs after the December 31, 2010, sunset date, this latter provision is, in effect, nullified.)

> ### Observation
>
> It is possible to completely avoid estate tax for a QDOT established before 2010 where the surviving spouse dies in 2010 or thereafter. QDOTs, therefore, should be considered for use in the estate plan of any person married to a non-U.S. citizen.

Stock Option Trust

Consider putting some or all of your nonqualified stock options in trust for your children. Although you must pay income tax on the value of the options when they are exercised, you could save a substantial amount of estate and gift tax. Most option plans may need to be amended to allow this type of transfer.

Effect of Reduced Tax Rates on Dividends

The reduced income tax rates (15 percent or 5 percent) on capital gains and dividends (see Chapters 1 and 2) also apply to trusts. The lower income tax rates on dividends are particularly beneficial for dividends that are retained by and taxed to a trust because the trust income tax brackets are extremely compressed—for 2005, trust income above $9,750 is taxed at the highest rate of 35 percent (compared to married individuals filing jointly, who do not reach the 35 percent bracket until their income exceeded $326,450).

Many trusts give the trustee the discretion to distribute income to
beneficiaries (in which case the income is generally taxable to the
beneficiaries) or to retain the income in the trust (in which case the
income generally is taxable to the trust).

The relative tax brackets of the trust and the beneficiaries frequently are a factor used by a trustee in deciding whether to make
distributions to the beneficiaries. In the past, retained dividends
may have been taxed at the highest tax rate due to the compressed
income tax brackets for trusts. Conversely, if the trustee distributed
the dividends to the beneficiaries, this income may have been taxed
at a lower tax rate because the beneficiaries may not have been in
the highest income tax bracket.

The reduction in the income tax rate on dividends for both trusts
and individuals generally means that the dividends are taxed at the
same rate, whether or not they are distributed from the trust. This
should allow the trustee to decide whether to make distributions
based on other factors, such as the needs of the beneficiaries, or
the grantor's original purpose in establishing the trust.

Trustee's Investment Decisions

The reduction in the income tax rate on dividends gives the trustee
an additional factor to consider in making investment decisions for
the trust. For example, in the past, interest and dividends generally
were taxed at the same rate. Therefore, a trustee may have decided
to invest the trust assets in a way that generated significant interest
income. Trustees now may need to consider whether the preferential treatment of dividends warrants a change to an investment strategy designed to produce less interest income and more dividend
income.

Allocation of Expenses

Generally, the trustee can choose how to allocate trust expenses
among the different categories of trust income (such as interest and

dividends). Since dividends and interest now will be taxed at different rates, a trustee should allocate expenses to income, such as interest, that is taxed at a higher rate.

Give a Roth IRA

Provide funds for a Roth IRA contribution each year to family members who have earned income and who do not exceed the income limitation for Roth IRA contributions (see Chapter 3). Providing the funds will be considered a gift to the family member, but unless other gifts have been made, this gift should qualify for the annual gift tax exclusion.

> ### Observation
> Gifts of IRA contributions are an excellent way for parents and grandparents to help their children and grandchildren accumulate significant retirement assets. The early start allows the tax-free compounding to build significant asset value.

Pay Gift Taxes Now

Under a peculiar quirk in the Tax Code, it can be less costly to pay gift taxes rather than to pay estate taxes after death. Individuals with large estates might consider making large gifts and paying significant gift taxes before death. You must survive at least three years after the payment of a gift tax to realize the savings. Not only will future appreciation escape estate tax, but also a lower overall transfer tax can result. With the prospect of estate tax repeal in 2010, however, the idea of paying any substantial amount of gift tax now becomes much less appealing. Very old or unhealthy taxpayers who are likely to live three years are the most likely candidates for this strategy.

Idea Checklist

☑ Review your will and estate plan to determine what adjustments are needed to benefit from changes to the estate and gift tax and to avoid potentially costly pitfalls. Especially consider whether you need to change or eliminate an existing credit shelter trust arrangement.

☑ Use asset ownership forms that maximize estate tax savings (such as limited liability companies or limited partnerships).

☑ Review the use of joint ownership.

☑ Make annual exclusion gifts each year ($11,000 per donee in 2005; $12,000 per donee in 2006).

☑ Gift appreciated capital assets to children and grandchildren in the lower tax brackets, so that they will be liable for only a 5 percent tax on their sale.

☑ Pay tuition expenses directly to an educational institution or make a payment to a health care provider. Consider a multi-year tuition gift, where appropriate.

☑ Move life insurance into a life insurance trust.

☑ Put rapidly appreciating assets into a grantor retained annuity trust or sell them to an intentionally defective trust.

☑ Reconsider the investment mix of trust assets to take advantage of lower dividends and capital gains tax rates.

☑ Set things up to take advantage of any available valuation discounts.

The bottom line is that Congress has opened a window of opportunity for taxpayers to optimize their estate and gift planning. It is important to take advantage of these opportunities as soon as possible.

Chapter 8

CHARITABLE GIVING

Before discussing the different charitable giving vehicles, it is necessary to examine the tax rules governing charitable deductions, including gifts that qualify for the deduction, as well as timing issues, valuation issues, and qualified charitable organizations.

The Charitable Deduction

To benefit from a gift of a charitable contribution, donors must itemize deductions on their tax return. Specific rules relating to donations determine whether a deduction can be claimed for a charitable contribution. A charitable deduction will be allowed only after the rights of actual possession in the donated property shift from the donor (and those parties related to the donor) to a qualified charitable organization. In addition, specific tax rules relate to donations of tangible personal property as well as to the type of charitable organization receiving the donation.

A contribution is considered made when delivery occurs. For example, mailing a check to a charitable organization constitutes an effective contribution on the date of delivery or mailing (identified by the postmark date). As a result, a check mailed as late as December 31 will qualify the gift for a charitable deduction for that tax year. Similarly, a gift of a properly endorsed stock certificate will be considered completed on the date of delivery or mailing to the charity. Alternatively, if the stock certificate is delivered to a broker or the issuing corporation, the gift will be completed on the date the stock is transferred on the books of the broker or issuing corporation.

Payment by credit card of a charitable contribution is deductible by the donor on the date the payment is charged to the credit card, rather than the date the authorization to charge is mailed to the charity. A pledge to make payment to a qualified charitable organization, however, generally is not deductible until payment has been made by any of the methods discussed.

Charitable Contributions

The Tax Code provides little guidance in defining the term "charitable contribution." It states that a charitable contribution is a contribution or gift to certain enumerated organizations (generally known as Section 501(c)(3) organizations), which are organized and operated exclusively for religious, charitable, scientific, literary, or educational purposes or to governmental units or entities for a public purpose. Each year, the IRS issues a list of qualified charitable donees in Publication 78, "Cumulative List of Organizations Described in Section 170(c) of the Internal Revenue Code."

The IRS uses a portion of its web site (http://www.irs.gov) to list qualified charitable organizations. Once on the IRS web site, type "Publication 78" in the search box and you will be directed to the online version of IRS Publication 78, the list of qualified charitable organizations. The organizations listed by the IRS have generally obtained an exemption letter from the IRS that verifies their tax-exempt or "Sec. 501(c)(3)" status. Certain charitable organizations, such as churches or smaller charities, however, need not obtain an exemption letter from the IRS.

For a contribution to qualify for a charitable deduction, there must be a gift. A gift is generally defined as a transfer of something of value with no consideration given or expected in return. Thus, if there are "strings" attached to a donation, it may not qualify as a gift. In addition, donative intent is an important element of a charitable contribution. The courts and the IRS will look for such factors as a lack of consideration expected or received (i.e., no quid pro quo) and for "detached and disinterested generosity."

Deductible Contributions—Quick Guide

Contributions of money or property are generally deductible if given to:

- Churches, synagogues, temples, mosques, and other religious organizations.
- Federal, state, and local governments if made solely for public purposes (e.g., a gift to reduce the public debt).
- Nonprofit schools and hospitals.
- Public parks and recreation facilities.
- Salvation Army, Red Cross, CARE, Goodwill Industries, United Way, Boy Scouts, Girl Scouts, Boys and Girls Clubs of America, and so on.
- War veterans' groups.

In addition, charitable deductions may be taken for expenses paid for a student living with the donor, sponsored by a qualifying organization, and out-of-pocket expenses paid by a donor who serves a qualified organization as a volunteer if certain conditions are met.

Nondeductible Contributions—Quick Guide

Contributions are *not* deductible if made to:

- Political action committees.
- Social and sports clubs.
- Chambers of commerce.
- Trade associations.
- Labor unions.

- Certain social welfare organizations.
- Most foreign charities.
- Political parties.
- Organizations that primarily engage in lobbying activities.
- Other nonqualified organizations.

In addition, payments made for tuition; raffle; bingo or lottery tickets; and dues, fees, or bills paid to country clubs, lodges, fraternal orders, or similar groups; as well as the value of a donor's time or services or value of blood given to a blood bank are all not deductible as charitable contributions.

A charitable organization that provides goods or services to the donor in exchange for a contribution in excess of $75 is required to furnish a written statement to the donor of the deductible amount and a good faith estimate of the value of the goods or services provided.

Valuation Issues

A donation that qualifies as a charitable contribution must be valued in order to determine the deductible amount. Valuation is the responsibility of the donor who is claiming the charitable contribution deduction. Proper valuation is doubly important because undervaluing a contribution will reduce the available charitable deduction, but overvaluing could subject the donor to additional taxes, interest and penalties.

For contributions of cash, value simply equals the dollar amount donated. For contributions of property, valuation becomes more difficult. IRS regulations state that charitable contributions of property, other than money, will be valued at "fair market value" at the time of the contribution, subject to certain reductions discussed below. "Fair market value" is defined as "the price at which the property would change hands between a willing buyer and a willing seller, neither being under any compulsion to buy or sell." Encumbrances or debts on such property will also affect the value of the contribution and the tax consequences to the donor.

In determining the fair market value of donated property, one or more of four different factors are most often used. They are *opinions of experts, cost or selling price, sales of comparable properties,* and *replacement cost.* See Table 8.1 on page 162 for questions the IRS indicates you should consider when using these factors for valuing property contributed to a charitable organization.

Listed next are valuation guidelines for different types of assets:

Assets	Valuation Guidelines
Cash	Amount donated
Retail property	Retail price
Stocks and bonds	Exchange price
Closely held businesses	Appraised value (could be subject to "discounting")
Notes	Unpaid balance plus interest
Life insurance	Cost/replacement cost
Real estate	Appraised value (comparable sale, capitalization of income, or replacement cost)
Artwork	Appraised value (or cost if donated by artist)

The following discussion describes the valuation rules for several types of property that are commonly contributed to charity.

Property Available to the Public at Retail

For purposes of charitable contributions, the value of property generally sold to the public equals the price at which the property would be sold at retail. For example, a passenger van donated by an individual to a charitable organization to be used by that organization to

Table 8.1   *Determining Fair Market Value*

When Using This Factor	Questions to Consider
Opinions of experts	Is the expert knowledgeable and competent?
	Is the written opinion thorough and supported by facts and experience?
Cost or selling price	Was the purchase or sale of the property reasonably close to the date of contribution?
	Was any increase or decrease in value, as compared to actual cost, at a reasonable rate?
	Do the terms of purchase or sale limit what can be done with the property?
	Was there an arm's length offer to buy the property close to the valuation date?
Sales of comparable properties	How similar is the property sold to the property donated?
	How close is the date of sale to the valuation date?
	Was the sale at arm's length?
	What was the condition of the market at the time of sale?
Replacement cost	What would it cost to replace the donated property?
	Is there a reasonable relationship between replacement cost and fair market value?
	Is the supply of the donated property more or less than the demand for it?

fulfill its charitable purpose would be valued at the price the van would sell to the general public, rather than to an automobile dealer.

Stocks and Bonds

Contributions of stocks and bonds are valued at the fair market value of the stock or bond as of the date of the gift. For stocks and bonds traded on a stock exchange or other public market where values can be easily ascertained, the fair market value is the average between the highest and lowest selling prices on the date of the contribution. If the stock or bond was not traded on the date of contribution, but was traded within a reasonable period of time before and after that date, the donor would use a weighted average of the highest and lowest selling prices before and after the date of contribution. You can also use the weighted average where the stock or bond was not traded within a reasonable amount of time, or you can use bona fide bid-and-ask prices on the date of the contribution.

Interests in Closely Held Businesses

Contributions of interests in a closely held business pose particularly difficult valuation problems. The IRS often employs a "willing buyer/willing seller" analysis to determine value but provides that the following additional factors should be used in valuing the business interest:

- A fair appraisal as of the date of the contribution of all tangible and intangible (including goodwill) assets of the business;
- The demonstrated earning capacity of the business; and
- The dividend-paying capacity, the economic outlook of the industry, the company's position in the industry, the degree of control of the business represented by the block of stock to be valued, and the value of any other comparable business whose stock is traded on a stock exchange.

> **Observation**
>
> The practice of "discounting" (reducing the value to reflect the lack of control connected with minority interests or lack of marketability of nonpublicly traded stock) has become a popular technique to reduce gift or estate tax liability. It is possible that the IRS may apply the concept of discounting the value of a charitable gift to "discount" the value of charitable donations of such stock. Charitable gifts of closely held stock will likely receive more IRS scrutiny due to the inherent valuation concerns. Care should be taken to ensure that proper valuation procedures are followed. Generally, an outside appraisal by a qualified appraiser is obtained in this context.

Interests in Notes

The fair market value of any note is calculated by adding the unpaid balance and the accrued interest to the date of the contribution. The donor may be required to report a different value if there are factors to warrant an alternative valuation. Such factors include interest rate fluctuations, the ability to collect on the note, and the fact that the property pledged as security is insufficient to satisfy the obligation.

Interests in Life Insurance

The valuation of contributions of life insurance can depend on whether the insurance policy has been paid in full at the time of the contribution. The fair market value of a single premium policy transferred immediately after payment is the cost of the policy. The fair market value of a paid-up insurance policy is the amount that the issuer of the policy would charge for a similar policy of the same specified amount on the life of a person who is the same age and health as the insured at the time of the contribution.

For contributions of insurance policies with premiums still due, determination of the fair market value is more complex. Typically, the issuing company can assist donors of unpaid insurance policies in determining the fair market value for charitable contribution purposes. Any additional premium payments will result in additional charitable contributions that are deductible in the year paid.

Interests in Real Estate

Contributions of real estate often present unique valuation problems. Competent appraisers are needed to determine the fair market value for charitable contribution purposes. Generally, real estate is appraised using one of three valuation methods or a combination of these methods. The comparable sale method compares the donated property to other similar properties that have been sold. Such factors as the time of prior sales, location of properties, and interest rates need to be considered in valuing donated real estate. Other methods of valuation include the capitalization of income method, which incorporates an analysis of the present value of income to be produced in the future, and the replacement cost method, which determines the cost required to replace the donated property.

Contributions of real property subject to a mortgage are deductible only up to the amount of value in excess of the mortgage.

Paintings, Antiques, and Other Objects of Art

For deductions of over $5,000, contributions of paintings, antiques, and other objects of art should be supported by a written appraisal from a qualified and reputable source. A claim for a deduction of

$20,000 or more must be accompanied by a complete copy of the signed appraisal attached to the donor's tax return. For individual items valued at $20,000 or more, a photograph of a size and quality that fully shows the object must be provided if requested.

For artwork that has been appraised at $50,000 or more, the donor may request a *Statement of Value* for the item from the IRS.

Caution

The donor must pay a user fee of $2,500 for a *Statement of Value* for one to three items of art. This fee is not refundable unless the IRS refuses to issue the *Statement of Value* "in the interest of efficient tax administration."

Jewelry and Gems

An appraisal by a specialized jewelry appraiser is almost always required for valuation of a donation of jewelry or a gem. The appraisal should describe (among other things) the style of the jewelry, the cut and setting of the gem, and whether it is still in fashion. The stone's color, weight, cut, brilliance, and flaws should be reported and analyzed.

Observation

Sentimental personal value has no effect on the value of the jewelry. However, if the jewelry is or was owned by a famous person, its value might increase.

Cars, Boats, and Aircraft

The 2004 Act changed the treatment of charitable donations of cars, boats, and airplanes. If the vehicle is sold by the charity, the charitable contribution will be limited to the gross sales proceeds that the charity receives upon the sale of the car, boat, or airplane. If the charity sells the property, it is now obligated to report to the taxpayer within 30 days of sale the amount of proceeds realized on the sale. This new valuation rule does not apply if the vehicle is used substantially for charitable activities.

If the vehicle is not sold by the charity prior to significant charitable use, the fair market value can be deducted. Commercial firms and trade organizations publish periodic guides to dealer sale prices for recent model years of cars and other vehicles. These prices are not "official" for valuing specific donated property, but they do provide clues for making an accurate appraisal of fair market value. The IRS has indicated it will continue to closely examine values and donors should carefully consider this in making a final determination of value.

Used Clothing and Household Goods

The value of both used clothing and household goods is usually much lower than the price paid when new. The price that buyers of used items actually pay in stores selling these goods, such as consignment or thrift shops, is an indication of fair market value.

Hobby Collections

Collectibles are often the subject of charitable donations. Most common are rare books, stamps, coins, natural history items, manuscripts, autographs, and so on. Many of the rules applicable to paintings and other objects of art (discussed previously) also apply to miscellaneous collections. Publications are often used to help determine the value of many types of collections.

Observation

Be certain to use the current edition at the date of contribution of these price guides. These sources are not always reliable indicators of fair market value and, where the collection has significant value, should be accompanied by an appraisal from an expert.

Appraisals and Substantiation Requirements

Any charitable deduction claimed in connection with a contribution of property valued in excess of $5,000 ($10,000 for gifts of closely held stock) from an individual, closely held corporation, partnership, or S corporation must be supported by a qualified appraisal. This rule does not apply to publicly traded securities.

For gifts of closely held stock not requiring an appraisal, a partial summary of the property is required. If a deduction of $20,000 or more is claimed for a contribution of art and for any noncash contribution in excess of $500,000, a complete copy of the signed appraisal must be attached to the tax return.

IRS Form 8283 has been designed to provide this information. This form is required to be signed by the appraiser and a representative of the charity, when an appraisal is required. The IRS can disallow a charitable deduction if a required appraisal is not secured. A "qualified appraiser" is generally someone who holds himself or herself out to the public as an appraiser, or performs appraisals on a regular basis, and has qualifications to value the particular type of donated property.

The weight given to an appraisal depends on the completeness of the report, the qualifications of the appraiser, and the appraiser's demonstrated knowledge of the donated property. An appraisal must give all the facts on which to base an intelligent judgment of the value of the property.

> ### Observation
>
> The IRS may accept the claimed value of the donated property, based on information or appraisals sent with the return, or may make its own determination of fair market value.

> ### Observation
>
> A charitable deduction may not be taken for fees paid for appraisals of donated property. However, these fees may qualify as a miscellaneous deduction (subject to the 2 percent limit) on Schedule A (Form 1040) if paid to determine the amount allowable as a charitable deduction.

The substantiation rules and IRS enforcement have become stricter. No deduction is allowed for any contribution in excess of $250 that is not substantiated by the charitable organization. The substantiation statement must indicate the amount of the contribution and the value of any goods or services provided to the donor. For single contributions in excess of $250, a canceled check is not considered a valid form of substantiation. When the value received by the donor in connection with any contribution exceeds $75, such as a dinner dance sponsored by a charity, the charitable organization is required to inform the donor of the value of any goods or services received, so that the donor can adjust the amount of the contribution by the value of the benefit to the donor.

Penalties for Overvaluation

Penalties assessed for overstating the value of a charitable contribution can be quite severe. The portion of the underpayment attributable to the valuation misstatement must exceed $5,000 for the penalty to be assessed. If the value reported on a donor's tax return is 200 percent higher than the actual value, the IRS will subject the taxpayer to a penalty equal to 20 percent of the portion of the underpayment. If the valuation misstatement is deemed "gross" (reported value is 400 percent greater than the actual value), the penalty is equal to 40 percent of the underpaid tax.

There is a reasonable cause exception to this penalty. For valuation misstatements related to charitable contribution property, the donor must prove that the value claimed was based on an appraisal performed by a qualified appraiser and that the donor made a good faith investigation of the value of the donated property.

Reduction of Contribution Amount

Sales of certain property held for longer than one year will produce long-term capital gains. A contribution of this type of property to certain charities (rather than a sale of the property) usually generates a deduction equal to the fair market value of the donated property. In addition, a contribution, rather than a sale, avoids recognition (and tax) of any gain. This provides an obvious incentive for a donor to contribute appreciated long-term capital gain property to a charity rather than to sell the property and donate the proceeds.

> **Observation**
> Note that the opposite strategy applies to property that has declined in value. It generally would be more beneficial to first sell the property and recognize any potential loss, and then donate the cash proceeds to charity.

The income tax law and related regulations require certain charitable contributions to be reduced in value when determining the amount of the available charitable deduction. In effect, these rules prevent a donor from claiming the full fair market value deduction as explained previously.

Contributions of ordinary income property (defined as property that would not produce long-term capital gains if sold at the time of the contribution) must be reduced in value for charitable deduction purposes. Examples of this type of property include inventory, a work of art created by the donor, and letters and memoranda written by the donor. In addition to ordinary income property, contributions of short-term capital gain property (property held for not more than one year) must be reduced.

The reduction rules require that a deduction for donated property be reduced by the amount of gain that would not have been long-term. In effect, the rules require donors to use their tax basis in the property, rather than the fair market value, to determine the charitable deduction. These reduction rules also apply to contributions of tangible personal property if the property is unrelated to the exempt function of the charitable organization and to gifts of long-term capital gain property, other than qualified appreciated stock, if the gift is to or for the use of a private foundation. The exception for "qualified appreciated stock" applies for gifts made of publicly traded stock of which not more than 10 percent of the total is owned by family members. Thus, gifts of closely held stock to a private foundation are subject to this reduction rule.

Percentage Limitations

After determining that a transfer of property is a contribution eligible for a charitable deduction, a donor often is surprised to find out that there are limits on the amount eligible for the deduction. These limitations are based on an individual's annual contribution base, generally equal to the individual's adjusted gross income

(AGI). The limitations in Table 8.2 are calculated based on the characterization of the charitable organization receiving the contribution (public charity versus private foundation) and the type of contributed property (long-term versus short-term capital gain property and ordinary income property). Again, the rules are complex and this discussion has been simplified. Donors should consult with their tax professionals prior to making substantial charitable contributions.

Private Foundations

A private foundation is a tax-exempt organization that is organized and operated exclusively for religious, charitable, scientific, literary, or educational purposes and does not meet the requirements that would classify it as a public charity. Both private foundations and public charities are called "Section 501(c)(3)" organizations.

Every tax-exempt charitable organization is classified as a private foundation unless it receives broad public support, or is a church, school, hospital, or organization operated to support another public charity.

A private foundation often is established by an individual or family. In addition, many corporations establish foundations in their names.

It should be noted that like the increased scrutiny of charitable gifts, the IRS has stepped up its review of private foundations to ensure that no inappropriate acts of "self-dealing" between donors and their private foundations exist. Careful analysis should be given to such limitations before a private foundation is implemented.

Nonoperating Foundations

Most private foundations do not actively conduct their own charitable activities, such as operating a museum or nursing home, and

Table 8.2 *Percentage Limitations*

Type of Gift	Deductible Amount	AGI Limitation	
		Public Charity[1]	Private Foundation (PF)
Cash	Fair market value	50 percent	30 percent
Ordinary income property: • Inventory • Short-term capital gain property • Depreciable property	Lesser of fair market value or adjusted basis	50 percent	30 percent
Appreciated long-term capital gain property	Fair market value except: • Certain contributions to a PF-limited to adjusted basis • Personal property not related to tax-exempt purpose—limited to adjusted basis	30 percent[2]	20 percent
Publicly traded stock	Fair market value	30 percent	20 percent
Carryover		5 years	5 years

[1] Private operating and passthrough private foundations are subject to the same AGI limitations as public charities.
[2] The donor may elect to apply the 50 percent-of-AGI limitation by decreasing the deductible amount for any potential long-term capital gain. The election applies to all gifts given that year.

These percentage limitations apply to contributions made directly "to" charities. Lower percentage limitations may apply to contributions made "for the use of" charities (such as contributions to some trusts).
For estate purposes, there are no limitations on the deduction available to a decedent's estate. All contributions made by bequest are deductible based on the property's full fair market value.

therefore are classified as "nonoperating." These foundations are required to make distributions equal to at least 5 percent of the fair market value of their assets each year. The charitable contribution deduction for an individual to a nonoperating foundation generally is limited to 30 percent of the individual's AGI for gifts of cash and 20 percent for gifts of appreciated property such as stock.

Operating Foundations

An operating foundation is one that actively conducts a program of charitable activities, rather than merely providing passive support to other charities. Individuals can claim a charitable deduction of up to 50 percent of AGI—the same as public charities for contributions to these entities. Usually, operating foundations are museums, libraries, or care facilities for the elderly.

Passthrough Private Foundations

If a private foundation distributes all of its annual gifts plus its investment income in any given year, the higher 50 percent AGI limit applies. The decision to make distributions and achieve passthrough status can be changed from year to year.

Tax Compliance and Operating Rules for Private Foundations

Private foundations file tax returns annually to report their activities. Most foundations will pay a 2 percent excise tax on their net investment income including realized capital gains. In some instances, it is possible to reduce the excise tax to a 1 percent tax rate.

Failure to follow the tax rules associated with the operations of a private foundation can subject the founder and the foundation itself to severe penalties.

Alternatives to Private Foundations

Because of the rather strict rules that apply to private foundations, some donors desire alternatives to a private foundation:

- *Community foundations.* A community foundation is a fund that is designed to attract assets for the benefit of a particular geographic area. Community foundations are treated as public charities (not as private foundations), so the donor has a large degree of flexibility both in structuring the gift and in advising the foundation on how to benefit the surrounding community. Because the community foundation is a public charity, there are no excise taxes to worry about.

- *Supporting organizations.* A supporting organization is similar to a private foundation in that typically it is privately organized and the donor retains some influence over the organization. To qualify for public charity status, it must support a named, publicly supported charity.

- *Donor-advised funds.* This is another way of retaining a degree of control over contributions. Generally, a public charity establishes such a fund and allows the donor to serve on an advisory board or to make "suggestions" as to the use of funds. Some mutual fund families have established donor-advised funds that facilitate charitable giving.

Observation

Donor-advised funds have become a popular way to contribute to charitable organizations and maintain a continuing active role in how the contributions are used. A donor-advised fund or group of funds is established by a public charity, and allows the donor or the donor's family to give advice or make recommendations regarding distributions made by the fund.

These funds are an alternative to establishing a private foundation, and avoid the record keeping, filing, and other administrative chores associated with private foundations. The funds can generally be established with smaller contributions than would be needed to justify the expense of maintaining a private foundation. Excise taxes that can apply to private foundations also do not apply to donor-advised funds. In addition, contributions to donor-advised funds are deductible as contributions to public charities, and, therefore, aren't subject to the lower limits that apply to private foundation contributions.

Although donors and their families may recommend how distributions from these funds should be made, the public charity that maintains the fund must have final decision-making authority. In practice, however, donors' wishes are taken very seriously by these funds. In the past few years, commercial investment firms have established charitable organizations to maintain donor-advised funds, which have attracted billions of dollars of contributions. The commercial funds benefit from their sponsors' investment experience, and the sponsors derive significant fees for their services.

Currently, guidance is lacking on the extent to which donors may be involved in decision making, and the IRS has not been vigorous in enforcing limits. However, there is a growing perception by the IRS that abuses do exist, and future guidance may rein in some of the more aggressive practices related to donor-advised funds.

The 50 Percent Limitation

As noted earlier, charitable contributions made to public charities (publicly supported charities, such as churches, hospitals, and educational organizations) and certain private operating foundations may be deductible up to 50 percent of a donor's contribution base. For charitable contributions that are greater than this base, the excess may be carried forward and deducted in the five tax years succeeding the year of the original contribution. The amount carried forward is subject to the 50 percent limitation of the donor's contribution base for each subsequent year a deduction is claimed.

For example, assume a couple has AGI (contribution base) of $200,000. In that tax year, they make a $125,000 cash donation to a university as part of its capital campaign. If the couple made no other charitable contributions in that tax year, they could deduct $100,000 (50 percent of the contribution base) and carry forward the remaining $25,000 to be deducted over the next five years, subject to the 50 percent limitation on each succeeding year's contribution base.

The 30 Percent Limitation

Cash contributions to charitable organizations (generally, private foundations) that are not designated as 50 percent organizations are deductible up to 30 percent of a donor's contribution base. In addition, charitable contributions of long-term capital gain property to public charities are subject to the 30 percent limitation. If a donor uses up more than 20 percent of AGI with cash contributions to public charities, the 30 percent limitation must be reduced so that the aggregate amount of contributions does not exceed the 50 percent limitation.

There is an alternative to the treatment of gifts of long-term capital gain property. This alternative allows donors to use the 50 percent limitation if they deduct an amount equal only to their tax basis rather than using the 30 percent limitation. This election should be used cautiously because it will apply to all such property that has been carried forward from prior tax years.

The 20 Percent Limitation

The 20 percent limitation applies to contributions of long-term capital gain property to private foundations. The 20 percent limitation is calculated in a similar manner to the 30 percent limitation in the previous example.

Other Alternatives

There are numerous other charitable giving vehicles that you may wish to consider such as charitable remainder trusts, charitable lead trusts, pooled income funds, and bargain sales. For a more complete discussion of charitable giving rules and alternatives, please consult *PricewaterhouseCoopers' Guide to Charitable Giving.*

YEAR-END TAX
SAVING STRATEGIES

Chapter 9

QUICK PLANNING GUIDE

Before the year closes, taxpayers have an opportunity to plan some moves that can cut taxes this year. To utilize year-end strategies, a taxpayer should have a good idea of his or her tax picture for this year as well as a good estimate of what it will likely be in the coming year. Changing tax rules make year-end planning more complex. Changes for the coming year, including new rules and inflation adjustments, must be factored in to any decisions.

What are the best year-end tax-saving strategies? They are those that produce the largest overall tax savings, taking 2005 and 2006 into account. There are three basic techniques:

1. Tax reduction.
2. Tax deferral.
3. Income shifting.

Tax Reduction

Tax reduction occurs when you take action that results in paying less tax than would otherwise have been due. For example, if you switch funds from a taxable investment (like a corporate bond) to a municipal bond that earns tax-free interest or to preferred stock that pays a dividend qualifying for a low tax rate, you will reduce your tax bill. Or you may want to consider contributing to a Roth IRA that can generate tax-free income instead of putting the money into a taxable investment vehicle. Another option is to shift funds from an investment, such as a money-market account or CD, which produces ordinary income, to a stock fund in hopes of earning some lower taxed dividends and long-term capital gain.

> ### Caution
> When doing your tax planning, don't forget about investment fundamentals. You want to find a prudent investment balance between risk and reward, taking into account your age, your family situation, and other factors. Taxes are important, but they're far from your only consideration. Work taxes into your overall financial plan, but don't let them be the driving force behind your decision making.

Tax Deferral

Tax deferral is achieved when you earn income now and pay tax on it in the future. Your retirement plan is an example. Although your retirement investments generate income throughout the years (with some years being unfortunate exceptions), they are generally taxed only when you receive them.

Deferring the receipt of taxable income can save you money, even if it produces little or no tax savings, because you can use your money longer before paying the IRS. That means greater compounding of earnings for you. On the other hand, accelerating income, even if you think you will be in a higher tax bracket in later years, means you will pay the IRS sooner than otherwise might be required. Loss of the use of that money cuts down on the advantage you hoped to attain.

Another deferral technique is to accelerate deductions from a later year to an earlier year so that you get their benefit sooner. But don't "over accelerate" deduction items to defer taxes. Remember that to get the deduction sooner, you usually have to lay out the dollars that fund the deduction sooner, which means you lose the use of those dollars. For example, an individual in the 35 percent tax bracket for 2005 and 2006 who accelerates a $5,000 deduction into 2005 defers $1,750 of tax. This may make economic sense if the deduction is shifted from January to December, but it is not beneficial for long periods because the funds you have to use to generate the deduction could lose more investment income in five months than the amount you would gain from accelerating the tax deduction at 35 percent for one year. Those in the lowest two tax brackets generally should not accelerate any deductions that could be paid later than February. If you are in the highest tax bracket, you should not accelerate expenses that could be deferred until May. Further care should be taken because not all expenses can be accelerated without limit. Also, moving up certain deductions, such as state income taxes, could trigger the alternative minimum tax (AMT) (see Chapter 12).

Observation

Sometimes a single move (see section on "Income Shifting" that follows) can combine tax reduction and tax deferral. By deferring income when tax rates drop from one year to the next, you will not only defer your tax liability, but you will also owe tax at a lower rate (assuming that your financial circumstances are about the same from year to year). Even without a year-to-year rate cut, you can achieve a similar result by shifting income to the later year if you expect to be in a lower tax bracket in the later year due to a change of circumstances, such as divorce or retirement.

Income Shifting

Income shifting generally involves transferring income-producing property to someone who is taxed at a lower rate. One example is giving a corporate bond to a family member who is in a lower tax bracket. For example, if you're in the 35 percent tax bracket for 2005, you will pay $350 in taxes on every $1,000 worth of taxable bond interest you receive. If you give the bond to a child or grand-child in the 10 percent or 15 percent tax bracket, tax on the interest will be cut to $100 or $150 per $1,000.

Observation

Qualifying dividends are taxed at only a 15 percent rate. And if the dividend-paying stock is transferred to a child in the 10 percent or 15 percent tax bracket, the dividends will be taxed at only 5 percent.

Caution

The so-called *kiddie tax* (which taxes children's investment income at their parents' tax rate) keeps this family income-shifting strategy from working for children under age 14. All but a small amount of the unearned income of a child under 14 is taxed at his or her parents' marginal tax rate.

Tax-saving techniques are described in Chapters 10 and 11. Before turning to these chapters, however, it is important to review how capital gains and the AMT affect your tax liability this year, when year-end tax saving strategies may work very well for you. For more details on accelerating deductions, see Chapter 10. For more on deferring income, see Chapter 11.

Year-End Capital Gains Checkup

2005 is a year in which many stock market investors experienced an up and down ride in the market.

Those who took profits on long-term gains will get the benefit of favorable capital gains tax rates. Investors whose gains are short-term are less fortunate. Their gains are taxed at regular income tax rates. If you have current capital losses, or unused capital losses carried over from earlier years, you may be able to get some tax advantages from them. You can offset capital gains—even short-term gains—and up to an additional $3,000 of other income with your capital losses.

For example, suppose you have a $10,000 gain on some stock in a company that has done well over the year, but that you think is due for a fall. If you sell some other stock at a $10,000 loss, you will be able to sell your gain stock and fully offset your tax liability with your loss. If you recognized a total of $13,000 of losses during the year, you could offset your $10,000 capital gain and use the extra $3,000 loss to offset $3,000 of other fully taxable ordinary income, such as interest or compensation income. If your excess losses come to more than $3,000, you have to carry them over to future years, when they can offset capital gains and up to $3,000 of ordinary income. (For more details about capital gains and losses, see Chapter 2.)

You have a great deal of flexibility at year-end to control the timing of investment decisions to maximize your tax savings. As year-end approaches, review your investment results. Calculate recognized gains and losses and compare them with unrealized gains or losses you currently hold. (See Chapter 2 for more information on netting capital gains and losses.)

If a taxpayer has potential capital losses exceeding capital gains realized for the year, he may want to use them to offset ordinary income to the extent of $3,000-receiving up to a 35 percent tax benefit-and wait to recognize additional long-term capital gains until

2006, when he will be assured of paying no more than a 15 percent rate on them.

As we said before, in making these tax decisions, you must also consider your individual financial and personal situation and the economic viability of particular investments. Taxes are but one factor to consider.

Year-End Alternative Minimum Tax Diagnosis

The AMT is a separate tax system under which certain items of income and deductions receive different—usually less favorable—tax treatment than under the regular income tax system. For example, state and local income taxes and real estate taxes are deductible under the regular system, but are not deductible under the AMT. The standard deduction, personal exemptions, some medical expenses, some interest on home-equity loans up to $100,000, and miscellaneous itemized deductions, which you can claim for regular tax purposes, don't reduce your AMT. Also, the bargain element (the difference between the exercise price and the stock's value at exercise) on incentive stock options (ISOs) that you exercise isn't subject to regular income tax in the year of exercise, but is subject to the AMT. You must calculate taxes under both systems and pay the higher tax bill. (For a more detailed explanation of the AMT, see Chapter 12.)

Planning for the AMT can be difficult because many factors can trigger it. If you believe that you are within range of becoming subject to the AMT, year-end strategies may help reduce your tax liability. If you are subject to the AMT, it may be prudent to go a counterintuitive route and do the opposite of normal year-end tax planning strategies. For example, individuals subject to the AMT might benefit from accelerating ordinary income items into 2005 and deferring until 2006 deductions that are not allowed for AMT purposes, such as taxes and miscellaneous itemized deductions.

If your 2005 year includes any of the items in the following list, you may need tax planning to avoid the AMT:

• Exercise of incentive stock options (as opposed to nonqualified stock options) for which the stock is held past December 31, 2005.

• Large prior-year state or local tax balance due, paid in April 2005.

• Large fourth-quarter state or local estimated tax payment that was made in January 2005 rather than in December 2004.

• Expenses that exceed 2 percent of income for investment management or tax-planning services or unreimbursed employee business expenses.

• Tax-exempt municipal bond income from private activity bonds.

• Business interests owned in S corporation or partnership form, in which these entities own significant amounts of depreciable assets.

• Large amounts of dividends or long-term capital gains.

• Interest on home-equity debt that is deductible for regular income tax purposes, where the borrowed funds were not used to improve the home.

• Passive activity losses that are allowable for regular tax purposes.

Now that the three basic tax-planning strategies have been reviewed, we move on to more sophisticated techniques, starting with accelerating deductions, which is the subject of Chapter 10.

Chapter 10
ACCELERATING DEDUCTIONS

Accelerating deductions into an earlier year gives taxpayers their benefits sooner. If tax rates are higher in the earlier year, the deduction also is more valuable because it offsets income that is taxed at a higher rate. That turned out to have been the case for deductions that were accelerated from 2003 into 2002. Since the lower tax rates are scheduled (absent future tax law changes) to continue to apply in 2006, accelerating deductions at the end of 2005 usually will generate only earlier—not larger—tax savings.

Nonetheless, those who expect to be in a lower tax bracket in 2006 for other reasons may get both tax benefits from accelerating their deductions into 2005.

Your goal is to use deductions to their full potential, keeping in mind that itemized deductions provide a tax benefit only if their total is more than the standard deduction amount.

Example
The standard deduction for a married couple filing a joint return for 2005 is $10,000. If you accelerate deductions from 2006 into 2005 and it turns out that your 2005 itemized deductions total less than $10,000, your effort won't have increased the amount

189

of deductions you can claim in 2005. In addition, you will have lost the opportunity to take that accelerated deduction in 2006 when it might reduce your taxes.

Equally important is something everyone knows but few act on: keep track of your deductions, as they occur, not six or seven months later. Nothing is more painful than trying to reconstruct legitimate expenses that are barely remembered. It is much easier to keep expense records current and ready for a running start on accelerating deductions.

If you determine that it pays to itemize deductions for the current year (based on the figures listed next), there are certain steps you can take to move up deductible expenses. As a general rule, you should pay deductible bills and expenses received this year, rather than waiting until next year to pay them. You should only defer the payment of a deductible expense if there is a clear benefit to the deferral.

If you want to move up deductions into this year, you can mail a check for a deductible item postmarked as late as December 31 and still claim it on this year's tax return, even though the check won't be cashed until next year. In the same way, deductible items charged on a credit card by year-end can generally be deducted on the current year's tax return, even if the credit card bill is not paid until the following year.

If your itemized deductions come close to the standard deduction amount each year (for 2005 the standard deduction is $10,000 for joint returns and $5,000 for singles), you can benefit by *bunching* itemized expenses in alternative years so that you can itemize every other year. Bunching strategies include planning to time the payment of larger charitable gifts, making January mortgage payments in December, accelerating or delaying the payment of real estate taxes and state and local income tax payments, and timing elective surgery and other medical expenses prior to year-end (though keeping in mind that cosmetic surgery is generally not deductible).

Observation

Deduction bunching works best for those who don't have recurring deductible expenses every year in excess of the standard deduction amount. For example, if you pay mortgage interest and state and local taxes each year that are more than your standard deduction amount, bunching may not help you. But if you have itemized deductions each year that are close to, but under, the standard deduction amount, bunching could work well for you. You might be able to itemize one year and claim the standard deduction the next, increasing your overall deductions and reducing your tax bills.

State and Local Taxes

State and local income taxes and real estate taxes are deductible in the year paid.

If you would benefit from accelerating deductions, consider December payments of state and local estimated taxes that are due in January. You also could move up the payment of any balance of state taxes due in April to the previous year-end, but it may be more beneficial to invest those funds for the 3½-month period, particularly if your marginal tax bracket is below 25 percent.

If you have an unusually large amount of taxable income in 2005, and will have a large balance due on your state or local return in April 2006, you should consider prepaying the amount in December 2005 so that you can "match" the state and local tax deduction with the income that generated it. This technique can help you avoid or minimize the impact of the AMT on your 2006 tax return. This is particularly so if your 2005 taxable income is expected to be substantially larger than in 2006 (perhaps because of an asset sold in 2005).

> **Caution**
> If you are subject to the alternative minimum tax (AMT) you
> will lose any tax savings that result from the deduction of state
> and local taxes because the deduction is not permitted in cal-
> culating the AMT. This means you will receive no tax benefit
> for an otherwise deductible expense.

Interest

You cannot deduct all interest paid on borrowed money. There are
six different kinds of interest expense for tax purposes—home mortgage (see Chapter 4), business, investment, passive activity, student
loan (see Chapter 5), and personal—and the deductibility of each
type is treated differently. Generally, the way borrowed funds are
used determines the category of the interest expense.

Business Interest

If you "materially participate" in the operation and management of
a passthrough entity (a partnership, LLC, or S corporation) or an
unincorporated business, you may generally fully deduct interest on
business-related borrowings.

> **Caution**
> For purposes of determining whether you can deduct interest,
> managing your investment portfolio is not considered a busi-
> ness. Deductibility of investment interest expense is more lim-
> ited, as discussed next.

Also, the IRS and most courts say that interest on a sole proprietor's
business-related tax deficiency is nondeductible personal interest.

Investment Interest

Interest on money that you borrow to purchase portfolio investments (such as stocks, mutual funds, bonds, and the like) that produce dividends, interest, royalties, or annuity income is deductible
only to the extent that the portfolio investments produce taxable income. You may carry forward indefinitely any excess investment interest expense and deduct it against your net investment income in
later years. To maximize your deductible investment interest, try to
match investment income with investment interest expenses. Note
that such interest is not deductible to the extent that the borrowing
was used to purchase or carry investments that produce tax-exempt
income (i.e., municipal bonds).

You can also elect to include long-term capital gains and/or qualified
dividend income as investment income against which investment interest may be deducted. If you make this election, however, these
gains and dividends will be taxed at ordinary income tax rates rather
than at the lower 15 percent (or 5 percent) capital gains tax rates.
The effect of the election is to save tax currently on your excess investment interest expense at the capital gains tax rate. This election
generally makes sense only when you expect to have excess investment interest expense for the foreseeable future.

Passive Activity Interest

Your share of interest incurred or paid on a passive activity investment is, in most cases, deductible only up to the amount of your income from all passive activities that year. A passive activity
investment is generally:

- An investment in an operating business in which you do not "materially participate."
- An investment in real estate or another "tax shelter." However,
  renting real estate to yourself or your business won't generate
  passive income. Generally, limited partnership investments are
  considered passive activities.

You may carry forward any excess passive losses and use them to offset passive activity income in future years. Also, you can usually deduct suspended passive losses from a particular passive investment in the year you sell your interest in the particular passive investment. When there is a complete sale (not a partial sale) or other disposition to an unrelated person of a passive investment in a taxable transaction, net passive losses are applied first against income or gain from other passive investments. Any remaining passive losses from the disposed passive investment are reclassified as nonpassive and can offset nonpassive income such as compensation income or portfolio income, including interest and dividends.

Example

In the year you sell your ownership interest in a real estate limited partnership, assume you have $10,000 of passive losses left after offsetting all available passive income for the year, including any gain from the sale of the real estate limited partnership. On your return for that year, you may deduct the $10,000 against your nonpassive income.

If your adjusted gross income (AGI) is under $100,000, a special exception permits you to deduct as much as $25,000 of passive rental real estate losses resulting from interest expense and other deductions if you "actively participate" in the management of the rental real estate. This exception phases out as AGI increases to $150,000. The active participation standard is much easier to satisfy than the material participation standard that generally is applied to determine whether an activity is subject to the passive loss limitations.

Example

You own a beach house that you rent out for the season each year. You have an agent who handles rentals, but you set the rental terms, approve tenants, make decisions involving maintenance and repairs, and hire contractors to do the work. Your personal use of the property is a very small percentage of the rental time. In this situation, you are an active participant in the rental real estate activity.

If your AGI is $100,000 or less, you may deduct up to $25,000 of losses from the rental real estate activity each year against your other nonpassive income. If your AGI is $125,000, you can deduct up to $12,500 of rental activity losses. In any year that your AGI is $150,000 or more, you cannot deduct any of the rental real estate losses against nonpassive income. Instead, the losses will carry forward to offset future passive income until the year of disposition.

There are even more liberal rules for investments in low-income housing and for individuals and closely held corporations that meet the definition of a "real estate professional." (See IRS Publication 527, "Residential Rental Property," for details concerning what it takes to qualify as a real estate professional.) Tougher rules apply to losses from interests in publicly traded partnerships. Losses from these activities can only offset income from the same activity until you dispose of the ownership interest in the activity.

The passive activity rules are extremely complex, and if you think you may be subject to them, you should consult your tax advisor.

Student Loan Interest

There is an above-the-line deduction (these deductions are sub-tracted directly from your gross income to calculate AGI)—available even to individuals who do not itemize deductions—for interest paid on a qualified education loan. The 2005 limit is $2,500 for interest paid on qualified education loans. The maximum deduction phases out for single taxpayers with an AGI between $50,000 and $65,000, and for married taxpayers filing jointly with an AGI between $105,000 and $135,000. These thresholds may be adjusted for inflation in coming years (see Chapter 5 for more details).

Observation

Many student loans have repayment terms that extend well beyond the five-year period that had limited deductibility in the past. The removal of the 60-month limitation means that interest on student loans is now deductible much more widely.

Example

You finished college with $30,000 in student loan debt, which you have arranged to repay over 10 years. Although you were a dependent of your parents while you were a student, you will no longer be claimed on their tax return. Previously, you would have qualified for the student loan interest deduction only for the first five years of interest payments. Now, however, you may deduct up to $2,500 of interest for each of the 10 repayment years, subject to the AGI limits.

Qualifying loans generally include only debt incurred solely to pay the higher education expenses for yourself, your spouse, or your children or grandchildren at the time the debt was incurred. Loans from relatives do not qualify. You must be the person legally responsible to repay the loan in order to deduct the interest. You can't deduct interest that you may pay, for example, on your child's loan. Nor can you deduct interest on a revolving credit line not earmarked specifically for higher education expenses. You are also not eligible for the deduction in years when you are claimed as a dependent on someone else's tax return.

Personal Interest

Interest incurred on car loans, credit cards, or IRS adjustments or any other interest falling outside the other five categories is generally not deductible. If you can obtain a favorable interest rate, you should consider taking out a home-equity loan to pay off any of these debts, because the interest on a home-equity loan of up to $100,000 can be claimed as an itemized deduction, except in certain situations for purposes of the AMT (see Chapter 4).

Medical Expenses

You can deduct unreimbursed medical expenses (including those of your spouse and dependents) to the extent that they exceed 7.5 percent of your AGI (10 percent for the AMT). Doctors' and dentists' fees, hospital bills, medical supplies, stop-smoking programs, and weight-loss programs to treat obesity, and prescription drugs are deductible to the extent not covered by insurance. In addition, your payments for health insurance and certain long-term care insurance (within limits) and long-term care expenses are included as medical expenses.

If medical expenses seem likely to be close to or exceed the 7.5 percent floor this year, consider accelerating elective treatment or surgery (keeping in mind that cosmetic surgery is generally not deductible as a medical expense) and paying for it before year-end. If the floor will not be reached this year but might be reached next year, consider the opposite strategy: delaying payment of medical bills whenever possible.

Observation

Although cosmetic surgery isn't generally deductible, the costs of reconstructive surgery and of radial keratotomy to correct vision without requiring prescription lenses are allowable medical expenses.

Other opportunities if you are self-employed include the following:
- Self-employed individuals may deduct 100 percent of the annual cost of health insurance for themselves, their spouses, and their dependents.
- This deduction is not allowed for months during which you are eligible to participate in an employer-provided health insurance plan (including your spouse's plan). Note that this deduction is an "adjustment to income" rather than an itemized deduction.

Therefore, it can be taken even by nonitemizers and is not reduced for itemizers at higher income levels.

- If you are self-employed, you may deduct a percentage of the
cost of long-term care insurance premiums, as long as you are not
eligible for any employer-provided long-term care insurance (including under your spouse's plan).

Charitable Contributions

Charitable contributions are one of the most flexible deductible
expenses, because you can usually control their timing and
amount.

For example, you could accelerate deductible expenses by making a
contribution in December rather than January. A contribution is
considered made at the time of delivery (mailing a check constitutes
delivery, assuming that it clears in due course). You cannot take a
deduction based only on a pledge—you must actually make the
contribution.

In general, you can deduct contributions to qualified public charities of up to 50 percent of your AGI. These deductions are also allowed for AMT purposes. Any excess can be carried forward for
five years.

Observation

Taking advantage of tax cuts may produce more disposable income that could be used to make charitable contributions. Alternatively, the tax rate reductions also remove some of the tax
incentive for charitable giving by increasing its after-tax cost.
Most charitable givers, however, have more than taxes in mind
when they make their contributions.

Observation

You can establish a donor-advised philanthropic fund as a means to get a current deduction and earn a tax-free return until you wish to donate the funds to particular charities. (See Chapter 8 for more information.) Donor-advised philanthropic funds can be established through community foundations as well as certain mutual fund companies and other financial and charitable organizations. The minimum contribution to establish the fund can be as low as $10,000.

Observation

Unreimbursed expenses you incur as a volunteer, including mileage driven in your car, are deductible. The mileage rate for purposes of the charitable deduction is 14 cents per mile for 2005.

Property Donations

Special rules apply to donations of property to charities. If you donate appreciated property, such as securities or land, your deduction is based on the property's current market value rather than on its original cost. Contributions of appreciated capital gains property, however, are limited to 30 percent of AGI unless a special election is made to reduce the deductible amount of the contribution.

Instead of selling property that has been held for longer than one year and has appreciated in value and then donating the proceeds, consider donating the property itself. If you sold the property and donated the proceeds, you would pay capital gains tax on any appreciation, while receiving a deduction for only the amount of cash that is left to contribute to the charity. If you donate appreciated property directly to a charity, you escape the capital gains tax and receive a deduction for the property's full fair market value.

If property that you are considering donating to charity has decreased in value, however, you should sell it and donate the proceeds. In addition to the charitable deduction, the sale will generate a capital loss that can be used to offset capital gains and up to $3,000 of other income each year. Any excess capital loss can be carried forward indefinitely.

For contributions of appreciated property to a private foundation, The restriction that used to limit the charitable deduction for gifts of publicly traded stock to your tax cost basis in the stock no longer applies. A full fair market value deduction for contributions of "qualified appreciated stock" is permitted. Such stock must be a long-term capital asset traded on an established securities market. No more than 10 percent of the value of all of a company's outstanding stock may be contributed.

Observation

The deduction for contributions of long-term capital gains property to a private foundation is generally limited to 20 percent of AGI for any year. Any excess can be carried forward and deducted for five years, subject to the 20 percent limit.

Any charitable contribution of property other than marketable securities that is worth more than $5,000 ($10,000 for gifts of closely held stock) must be supported by a qualified appraisal completed by the extended due date of your tax return. The appraiser and a representative of the charitable organization must sign Form 8283 or the deduction will be denied. Additional requirements apply to contributions of art if a deduction of $20,000 or more is claimed.

Substantiation Requirements

The general substantiation requirements for a deductible charitable contribution are:

- Cash contributions under $250. A canceled check is acceptable as long as no goods or services are received in exchange.
- Cash contributions of $250 or more. These contributions must be acknowledged in writing by the charity. You must obtain this documentation from the charity by the date your tax return is filed or the due date of the return (including any extensions), whichever is earlier. The acknowledgment must state whether the charity provided any goods or services in return for the contribution and, if so, provide the information required for quid pro quo contributions (see the following discussion).

Observation

This rule applies only if $250 or more is given at one time. For example, if over the course of a year, you make several contributions of $200 to the same charity, the substantiation requirement does not apply.

- Noncash contributions under $250. The donor should retain a detailed list of the items contributed, including the estimated value of the goods.
- Noncash contributions of $250 or more. The donor must obtain a receipt that describes the donated property (and indicates any goods or services received in exchange). The charity is not required to place a value on the property. For noncash contributions over $500, additional information must be included with the donor's tax return.
- Quid pro quo contributions over $75. A quid pro quo contribution is one that is partly a charitable contribution and partly a payment for goods or services. The charity must provide the

donor with a written statement that includes a good-faith estimate of the value of the goods or services provided and must in-
form the donor that the contribution deduction is limited to the
payment in excess of the value of the goods or services. Contributions are fully deductible if goods or services received from the
charity are only of nominal value or when only an intangible religious benefit is received.

Deferred Giving

The most common form of charitable contribution is the "current
gift," for which you transfer control of money or property to a charity and you keep no control over it.

In recent years, however, deferred giving has become increasingly
popular. This involves an irrevocable transfer to a charity whose ultimate use of the property is deferred to some time in the future.
For many, deferred gifts provide the best of all worlds: a current
charitable deduction, a retained income stream (or a future interest in the property for your beneficiaries), a charitable contribution
to a favorite organization, and a reduction in the donor's
taxable estate.

If you make substantial charitable contributions each year, consider
establishing a charitable lead trust or charitable remainder trust to
accomplish some of these desirable results. In a charitable lead
trust, you donate property to a trust that guarantees to pay the charity a fixed amount or a fixed percentage of the fair market value of
the trust's assets for a certain number of years. At the end of the
term, remaining trust assets revert to you or to a designated beneficiary, such as a child or grandchild.

In a charitable remainder trust, you transfer property to a trust, and
the trust guarantees to pay you or a designated noncharitable beneficiary a fixed amount or a fixed percentage of the fair market value
of the trust's assets for life or a term of years (not longer than 20

years). At the end of the term, the remaining assets are transferred to the charity.

Observation

The rules for establishing these charitable-giving vehicles are complex. If you are planning to make a large gift, contact your tax advisor to discuss how they work.

Caution

Deductions are not allowed for transfers to charitable organizations involving the use of split-dollar life insurance arrangements if the charity pays any premium for the donor. Employers often use split-dollar life insurance arrangements to provide a substantial amount of insurance coverage for key executives or employees. Split-dollar life insurance is permanent insurance purchased under an arrangement in which the company and the individual share the cost of the policy as well as its benefits and proceeds. (See Chapter 3 for more details.)

Casualty Losses

Observation

The past couple of years have had unusually high levels of hurricane devastation in the South. Hurricane Katrina in particular caused unprecedented damage and resulted in tax legislation designed to help survivors. Because of the narrow scope of the legislation, it is not discussed in this book. The one exception is on page 11, which applies to charitable contributions for all taxpayers.

If you have experienced a natural disaster or another sudden casualty and suffer property damage, a casualty loss deduction is available to help lessen the blow of any unreimbursed losses (casualty losses are deductible to the extent that they exceed any insurance reimbursement). In general, the amount of the loss is the lesser of the decrease in fair market value of the property or your adjusted basis (generally, your cost less depreciation deductions) in the property. Insurance reimbursements reduce the amount of the deductible loss. In addition, the first $100 of each loss is nondeductible. However, if several items are damaged or lost in the course of a single casualty, the $100 floor is applied only once. Finally, only total allowable casualty losses in excess of 10 percent of AGI may be deducted.

Example

Your home was severely damaged by a lightning strike, and your loss, after insurance reimbursement, is $20,000. The first $100 of the loss is not deductible. If your AGI is $70,000, $7,000 of the remaining $19,900 loss also is nondeductible. Thus, your casualty loss deduction would be $12,900 ($19,900 minus $7,000). If your loss occurs due to a presidentially declared disaster, such as an earthquake or hurricane, you can claim the loss either on your tax return for the year in which it occurred or on the prior year's return.

Observation

Claiming the loss on the earlier year's return (by filing an amended return, if necessary) may get you a refund faster, but the calculations need to be run both ways to see which choice results in the larger tax savings.

Miscellaneous Itemized Deductions

Certain miscellaneous expenses, mostly those related to employment, including job search expenses and investments (other than investment-related casualty and theft losses) are deductible only to the extent that they total more than 2 percent of your AGI. For example, if your AGI is $80,000, only miscellaneous itemized deductions totaling more than $1,600 are deductible.

Therefore, it may be desirable to "bunch" payment of these kinds of expenses to bring the total above the 2 percent floor at least every other year.

You can generally deduct (subject to the 2 percent floor) unreimbursed payments made in a given year for:

- The cost of unreimbursed job-related education or training.
- Unreimbursed business use of automobiles.
- Subscriptions to business or professional publications (including payment for next year's subscription).
- Membership dues in business or professional associations (including the following year's dues).
- Tax preparation and planning fees.
- Investment expenses, such as investment advisory fees or a safe deposit box.

If you receive tax preparation or investment advice or certain other financial services under a fixed-fee arrangement, you may be able to take deductions this year for payments covering a period that extends into next year. If you are delaying your deductions, you will want to make these payments after 2005.

Observation

Miscellaneous itemized deductions are not deductible in the AMT computation. Therefore, the AMT is a consideration when planning any acceleration of these deductions.

If you buy and sell securities, you should familiarize yourself with the definitions of *investor* and *trader*. The vast majority of individuals who buy and sell for their accounts are investors. Investors deduct their investment expenses as a miscellaneous itemized deduction, subject to the 2 percent floor and the itemized deduction phase-out at higher incomes. Traders, however, may deduct their expenses against their trading income. It is difficult to convince the IRS or the courts that you are a trader unless you regularly do a very large volume of short-term trades.

Moving Expenses

If you relocate because of a new job or business, you may be able to deduct certain moving expenses, including the costs of transporting household goods and traveling to your new residence. For these expenses to be deductible, your new job must be at least 50 miles farther from your former residence than your old job was from your former residence.

Several types of expenses associated with a move are not deductible, including: premove house-hunting expenses, temporary living expenses, the cost of meals while traveling or while in temporary quarters, and the costs of selling or settling a lease on the old residence or purchasing or acquiring a lease on a new residence. Employer reimbursements of deductible moving expenses are generally excluded from the employee's gross income, and deductible expenses not reimbursed by the employer are an "above-the-line deduction" instead of an itemized deduction.

Observation

Employers often reimburse all of their employees' moving costs, including any tax liability for moving expense reimbursements, when an employee is moved for the employer's convenience. Some of these reimbursements must be reported as taxable wages.

Above-the-line deductions are subtracted directly from your gross income to calculate AGI. They may be claimed both by itemizers and by those who take the standard deduction.

Depending on your situation, the following idea checklist may provide some help in reducing your tax bill.

Idea Checklist

☑ If your employer offers flexible spending accounts for medical or dependent care expenses, use them. These accounts allow you to pay these types of expenses with pretax dollars, offering real savings.

☑ If you have self-employment income and want to deduct contributions to a Keogh retirement plan, you must establish the plan by December 31, even though you can wait until the due date of your tax return (including extensions) to actually fund it. Alternatively, you may make deductible contributions to a simplified employee pension (SEP) plan, which can be both established and funded after December 31 (see Chapter 3).

☑ Evaluate your form of business entity. Net income from a sole proprietor business, a partnership, or an LLC may be subject to self-employment tax; however, not all income passed through from an S corporation is subject to the self-employment tax.

☑ Personal property taxes such as those required for automobile license plates or tags are deductible if they are ad valorem (i.e., based on the value of the property).

☑ Business owners can deduct only compensation that is deemed reasonable for services they and their family members provide.

☑ Corporate owner-employees should consider the impact of the reduced tax rate on dividends in deciding how much to take out of the corporation as compensation and how much as dividends (see Chapter 13).

This chapter described many tools and techniques that can help you use tax deductions at the end of 2005 and future years to lower your tax bills.

Chapter 11 sets forth a tax-planning strategy called *income deferral* that can be an important part of your overall tax-planning program.

Chapter 11
DEFERRING INCOME

Deferring income from one year to the next can be a very effective tax-planning strategy, especially for those in high tax brackets, because they will save the most. For tax purposes, many two-income families qualify as high-income individuals. Almost all individuals report their income and deductions using the cash method of accounting (in which income is reported in the year it is actually or constructively received, and expenses are deducted in the year they are paid), which gives quite a bit of flexibility in using tax-deferral strategies.

The key to saving from income deferral is that income is not taxed until it is actually or constructively received. For example, if a taxpayer does work for others, he or she will not be taxed until the year in which payment is received. So, deferring billing at year-end will result in more income being received and taxed in the following year. Some examples of situations in which income deferral may be useful follow.

Observation
Income deferral is even more valuable when income tax rates are scheduled to drop from one year to the next. Deferring income to a lower tax year not only delays payment of tax, but lowers the overall tax bill.

Year-End Bonuses

If you expect to receive a year-end bonus or other special type of lump-sum compensation payment, you may want to receive it and pay taxes on it in 2006 rather than in 2005. Your employer can probably still deduct the bonus in 2005 if the company is on the accrual method of accounting (which most larger companies are), as long as its obligation to pay you is established before year-end and payment occurs within 2½ months after year-end (March 15, 2006, for a calendar-year company).

Example

The company where you work uses the accrual accounting method, is on a calendar year, and has an incentive bonus program for which you qualify. In December 2005, the company's directors declare the bonus and set the amount of the payments, which will be paid on January 30, 2006. The result is that the company "accrues" its deduction in 2005 when it becomes liable for payment of the bonuses, but your tax liability is delayed until 2006.

Caution

This strategy of delaying payment of bonuses to the next year does not work for most payments to company owners: The company's deduction for payments to partners, S corporation shareholders, owner-employees of personal-service corporations, or shareholders who own more than 50 percent of a regular corporation is deferred until the year the bonus is actually paid to the owner—so the company is unable to accrue its deduction for the year in which the bonus was declared if it is not paid until the following year.

Deferred Compensation

You may want to consider an agreement with your employer so that part of your earnings for this year are paid to you in the future, perhaps over several years. This will delay your tax obligation. If you can wait until you are retired to receive the deferred compensation, you may be in a lower tax bracket, further reducing your tax bill on that income. In this type of arrangement, interest is often added by the company to compensate you for the delay in receiving the money. The 2004 Tax Act created strict new rules that must be followed in structuring deferred compensation agreements. Failure to follow these requirements will cause the employee to be taxed currently on the deferred compensation (with penalties).

The postponed compensation will not be taxed to you or be deductible by your employer until you actually receive it. But Social Security tax and Medicare tax are generally due when the income is earned regardless of when it is actually paid. If you are already over the FICA wage base for the year ($94,200 for 2006), you won't owe any additional Social Security tax, but you and your employer will each owe the 1.45 percent Medicare tax on the deferred amount. No additional Social Security or Medicare tax will be owed in the future when you receive the deferred compensation.

Caution

Today's low tax rates on compensation, dividends, and capital gains might cause executives to think twice before deferring salary or bonuses into nonqualified deferred compensation plans. Payments from a deferred compensation plan are treated as fully taxed ordinary income and tax rates may be higher at the time the payments are received. Thus, executives who elect to defer compensation forgo the opportunity to receive capital gains and dividends on investments they might have made with after tax dollars outside of the plan.

> ### Caution
> Executives also may question the premise that nonqualified deferred compensation provides an opportunity to shift income to retirement years, when they likely will be subject to a lower marginal tax rate. With marginal income tax rates relatively low from a historic perspective, executives also may question whether rates are likely to increase in the future, potentially subjecting their deferred compensation to higher tax rates at the time of distribution.

Unlike a qualified retirement plan, which generally must cover a broad range of employees, this nonqualified type of deferred compensation arrangement can usually be made for an individual employee. If you are interested in a deferred compensation plan, you should discuss it with your employer without delay because such a plan can only cover income you earn in the future, not that which you have already earned.

> ### Caution
> When you defer compensation, you are treated as a general creditor of your employer. If your employer goes into bankruptcy, you could lose your deferred compensation.

Stock Options or Stock Appreciation Rights

If you have nonqualified stock options or stock appreciation rights, in most cases, you will have taxable compensation income when you exercise them. Delay exercising them until next year if postponing income would be to your advantage.

Caution

By waiting to exercise their options, employees forgo the opportunity for capital gains on the underlying shares (any increase in the value of stock related to a nonqualified option will be taxed as ordinary income) and the right to receive dividends, both of which receive preferential tax treatment. However, they also receive the leverage effect of being able to participate in the appreciation in the underlying stock without committing capital (the exercise price). Therefore, despite the potential for lower tax rate dividends and capital gains, an analysis of exercise timing generally reveals that employees continue to be better off postponing exercise until later years. This may change, however, depending on assumptions regarding future income tax rates and the valuation behavior of the underlying stock.

If you have incentive stock options (ISOs), exercising them does not result in compensation income if the stock you acquire is held for the required periods (at least two years after option grant and one year after the option is exercised). If you meet these requirements, you generally won't owe any tax until you sell the ISO, and then your gain is taxed at favorable capital gains tax rates. But the spread between the option price and the fair market value at the time you exercise the option is added to your income for AMT purposes. (See Chapter 2 for a discussion of ISOs.)

Caution

If you are a "corporate insider" as defined under Securities and Exchange Commission rules, you should contact your financial and/or legal advisor, because you are subject to special limitations on the sale of your option stock. (See Chapter 2 for more details on stock options.)

Treasury Bills and Bank Certificates

If you invest in short-term securities, you can shift interest income into the next year by buying Treasury bills or certain bank certificates with a term of one year or less that will mature next year. If you buy a bank certificate, you must specify that interest be credited only at maturity.

Dividends

If you have a voice in the management of a company in which you own stock, you may want to take steps to see that dividends are paid in January 2006 rather than in late 2005. This will shift your tax liability on the dividends to 2006, since you won't receive the dividend income until the later year. This assumes that the preferential tax rate on qualifying dividends will not be legislatively repealed in 2006.

Installment Sales

You generally owe tax on profits from the sale of property in the year in which you receive the sale proceeds. To defer income from a sale of property, consider an installment sale, in which part or all of the proceeds are payable in the following year or later. In that case, tax will be owed as you receive the payments. Part of each installment payment you receive will be a tax-free return of your cost or basis, part will be interest income taxed at regular income tax rates, and part will be capital gain. Make sure that future payments are secured and that appropriate interest is paid on any unpaid balance.

> **Caution**
>
> If the property being sold has been depreciated, usually some of the gain will be taxed, or recaptured, at regular income tax rates. This recapture gain is subject to tax in the year of sale, even if you elect installment tax reporting. That is true even if

you don't receive any payment in the sale year. So, be sure to get enough up-front cash at least to cover your tax liability on recapture income.

You need not decide to report 2005 deferred payment sales on the installment method until you file your 2005 tax return (in 2006). This gives you more time to decide whether to be taxed on profits in 2005 or in 2006 and later years. If you choose not to report on the installment method, you must elect out of it. If you do elect out, you could be liable for tax on income that you will not receive until later years.

Caution

Special rules limit the use of the installment method. For example, inventory items and publicly traded stock do not qualify for installment-sale reporting. Also, installment notes in excess of $5 million may be subject to an interest charge.

U.S. Savings Bonds

Many people are aware that the interest earned on series EE U.S. savings bonds is tax-deferred for up to 30 years. However, many people are not familiar with the newer *series I U.S. savings bonds.* Series I bonds provide the same tax-deferral opportunities as series EE bonds. The major difference between these two bonds is the way the interest is calculated. Series I bonds pay an interest rate that is indexed for inflation.

Observation

The series I bonds are one of a very limited number of investments whose return is guaranteed to keep pace with inflation. Both EE and I bonds can be bought at your bank in various denominations. Purchases of these bonds are limited to $30,000 per person, per year.

Annuities

You can defer current investment income you now earn, such as stock dividends, bond interest, and interest on savings and money market accounts, by transferring the funds into deferred annuities, which shelter current earnings from tax. You won't owe tax on a deferred annuity until payouts begin. However, to get this benefit, you generally have to tie up your funds until you are at least 59½. Similar to IRAs, deferred annuities generate a penalty tax on premature withdrawals, subject to certain exceptions.

Caution

Since earnings from deferred annuities are subject to ordinary income tax when received, they don't benefit from reduced rates on dividend and capital gain income. There has always been a school of thought that only long-term periods of deferral would justify the use of deferred annuities (since they can convert lower tax-rate income into higher tax rate income). The reduced tax rate on dividends and long-term capital gains makes variable annuities invested in equities even less attractive.

For portfolios that produce significant short-term capital gains or ordinary income, however, annuities may remain attractive, especially for those far from payout status. And younger taxpayers should continue to consider these investments, since long periods of tax deferral may overcome the disadvantages.

Individual Retirement Accounts

If you earn compensation or self-employment income, you can establish a Roth IRA or a regular IRA, assuming you meet the income requirements. (See Chapter 3 for more information about IRAs.) Although your income level may disqualify you from getting the maximum benefits from these savings vehicles, you may still find some limited advantages. For example, even though you may not be able to deduct contributions to a regular IRA or qualify for the potential tax exemption of a Roth IRA, you may make nondeductible contributions to a traditional IRA no matter how high your income is and benefit from tax-deferred earnings until you withdraw your money, usually at retirement.

> ### Caution
>
> Like deferred annuities discussed above, the earnings from nondeductible traditional IRA contributions are subject to ordinary income tax when received, and therefore, don't benefit from reduced rates on dividend and capital gain income. However, if the scheduled "sunset" of the lower dividends and capital gains tax rates occurs in 2009, and these rates are not made permanent, taxpayers who passed on nondeductible IRAs for several years will not be able to make up those contributions.

401(k) Plans

401(k) plans are qualified retirement plans established by an employer under which employees can defer up to $14,000 of their compensation income in 2005 or $15,000 in 2006 (these limits are higher for those age 50 or older). As with an IRA, the earnings are not taxed until they are withdrawn. Contributions to these plans are made on a pretax basis, meaning that you aren't currently hit with income tax on the amount you contribute. That makes it easier for you to put more money into your account. (Social Security taxes, however, are owed on amounts you elect to defer to your 401(k) account.) Also, many employers match a portion of employee deferrals. Many 401(k) plans allow you to borrow from your accounts before retirement, if the loan is repaid on a regular schedule. (See Chapter 3 for further discussion of 401(k) plans.)

Shifting Income to Family Members

Shifting income to children or other family members in lower tax brackets is an excellent long-term planning strategy for high-income individuals. As a general rule, family income shifting should be done early in the year to get the most tax savings. It is never too early to begin planning for 2006 and later years.

Children age 14 or older are taxed at single individual tax rates (10 percent on the first $7,300 of taxable income and 15 percent on higher amounts up to $29,700 in 2005). You can also shift capital gains income from your 15 percent capital gains tax rate into a child's lower 5 percent tax rate (see Chapter 2).

The issue of who actually controls the funds—you or your child or grandchild—can determine the success of strategies that seek to use a child's lower tax rate. If you keep too much control over the transferred asset, the IRS may say you really haven't transferred it for tax purposes and will tax you on its income or sale.

The easiest way to effectively shift income is to use a custodial account, either a Uniform Gifts to Minors Act (UGMA) or a Uniform Transfers to Minors Act (UTMA) account. Keep in mind that state laws typically give the child access to UGMA/UTMA funds at age 18 or 21.

> ### Observation
> A few states, such as Alaska, California, and Nevada, allow these accounts to continue to age 25 under certain circumstances, as opposed to the cut-offs at 18 or 21 in most other states.

If you want to limit your child's access to the transferred assets beyond what an UGMA/UTMA account permits, consider a trust. But be wary of trust tax brackets. For 2005, the 15 percent bracket stops at $2,000 of taxable income, and the top bracket starts at $9,750. Also, trusts don't qualify for the 10 percent tax rate that applies for individuals. However, the new lower 15 percent tax rate on dividends and long-term capital gains, which applies to trusts as well as individuals, could mitigate most of the negative impact of these compressed tax brackets.

If you are planning to shift income to children under age 14, keep in mind that a kiddie tax is imposed on their unearned income (such as interest, dividends, and capital gains) over $1,600 in 2005. This income is taxable to the child at the highest tax rate of his or her parents. However, there are techniques that you can use to shift income to your children and avoid the kiddie tax.

You are permitted to shift enough assets to a child under the age of 14 to produce up to $1,600 of total 2005 unearned income (see Chapter 14 for the 2006 amount). The first $800 of that unearned income will be offset by the child's standard deduction, and the next $800 is taxed at the child's 10 percent rate.

Example

A six-year-old child has $2,000 of interest income in 2005 and no earned income. His or her 2005 standard deduction of $800 is allocated against his or her unearned income, and the remaining net unearned income is $1,200. The first $800 of the remaining $1,200 is taxed at the child's tax rate. The remaining $400 is taxed at the parents' top tax rate.

Unearned income	$2,000
Less: Child's standard deduction	−800
Remaining unearned income	$1,200
Less: Amount taxed at child's rate	−800
Remaining taxed at parents' top tax rate	$ 400

> ### Observation
>
> A transfer of assets that produces $1,600 of income to a child under the age of 14 can save a family in the 35 percent tax bracket $480 per year. When interest rates and investment rates of return are low, transfers of substantial assets can be made without going over the $1,600 unearned income limit. Note that asset transfers should be coordinated with the gift tax rules. (See Chapter 7 for a discussion of this strategy.)

Another technique is to transfer assets that generate little or no current taxable income. For example, consider giving a child under the age of 14:

- Growth stocks or growth-stock mutual fund shares.
- U.S. series EE and series I savings bonds (the interest on which may be tax deferred).
- Tax deferral products, such as annuities and variable life insurance contracts.
- Closely held stock of a C corporation.

These assets can be converted into investments that produce currently taxable income after the child is age 14 because income and any capital gains recognized on the conversion will be taxable at the child's tax rate, usually 15 percent for ordinary income and only 10 percent on the first $7,300 of taxable income in 2005 (see Chapter 14 for 2006 amount) and 5 percent (zero percent in 2008) for qualifying dividends and long-term capital gains.

> ### Caution
>
> Savings bonds held in your name may qualify for tax-free treatment when used to pay for your child's college education. If you transfer these bonds to your children, this exclusion will be lost. Because of income limitations on this tax-free treatment of

savings bonds, however, it is not available to high-income or many middle-income individuals. Even if loss of the education tax break isn't a factor for you, it is still a good idea to purchase new savings bonds for children rather than transferring your own bonds to them. That's because you would be taxed on the bond's accrued interest as of the transfer date. Unless the bonds are very new and the accrued interest amount is small, it is better to start with new bonds in the child's name.

Chapter 12 discusses a topic that has affected many more taxpayers than in prior years: alternative minimum tax. Even if you have not already been required to pay alternative minimum tax, there is an increasing likelihood that you will be paying alternative minimum tax in the near future.

Chapter 12
ALTERNATIVE MINIMUM TAX

The alternative minimum tax (AMT) is a parallel tax system to the regular income tax system, but generates an alternative tax liability by: applying different rules for determining alternative minimum taxable income; basically incorporating a flat tax rate; and limiting or eliminating the benefit of certain tax deductions and credits. As a result, the regular income tax rate reductions enacted in recent years are not fully realized by taxpayers who find themselves subject to AMT.

To avoid becoming an AMT victim, a taxpayer must first recognize that AMT planning is a complicated task that requires exceptional foresight. AMT planning might result in a suggestion that you accelerate your income and defer your deductions, which is in direct contradiction to familiar income tax planning practices.

An inadequate understanding of tax rules and their potential impact on your wealth goals and strategies could jeopardize your assets and long-term plans. Therefore, it is very important to explore and plan for the AMT by running your projected numbers under both the regular tax and AMT system for the current year and for several years into the future, focusing on the proper management of your overall tax liability for more than simply the current year.

In some instances, an AMT planning strategy may cause an increase in regular tax. Accordingly, a key factor to consider in AMT planning is the breakeven point where an individual's regular tax and AMT are approximately equal.

With diligent and thorough planning efforts, the effects of AMT can be lessened.

Understanding the Alternative Minimum Tax

As previously mentioned, the AMT is a separate, but parallel tax system to the regular income tax system. It has its own set of tax rates and its own rules for income and deductions, which are usually less generous than the regular rules. Both systems require a calculation of annual taxes, and the taxpayer must pay the tax under whichever system produces the higher amount. The AMT system includes, in general, a broader base of income due in large part to a smaller range of allowable deductions. Many favorable tax treatments available under the regular tax system are curtailed for the AMT by a system of adjustments and preferences. So, if you typically claim deductions, or have tax preference items or other adjustments, you may crunch the numbers under both regular tax and AMT and find that you are required to pay tax under the AMT system. Tax preference items or adjustments include, but are not limited to: state and local income taxes, real estate taxes, miscellaneous itemized deductions such as investment expenses and tax return preparation fees, certain tax exempt interest income, some depreciation expenses, the difference between AMT and regular tax gain on the sale of property, and nontaxable income on the exercise of incentive stock options.

Planning for AMT can be difficult because many factors can trigger it. If you believe that you are within the range of AMT, it may make sense to consider formulating year-end tax planning strategies geared toward reducing AMT rather than the regular tax. Again, the factors contributing to both regular tax and AMT must be considered.

AMT was first instituted in 1969 and was designed to ensure that high-income taxpayers, who had historically benefited from various tax preference items under the regular tax system, pay at least a minimum amount of tax each year. As mentioned, the AMT system acts on the premise that the taxpayer should pay the higher of the regular or minimum tax.

Today, stability more than anything has accounted for the increase in taxpayers being subject to the AMT. Inflation has been the real culprit of expanding AMT liability among taxpayers. The failure of Congress to adjust the base level of income that is exempt from AMT for inflation, together with the recent tax rate reductions, has dramatically increased the number of taxpayers subject to AMT. According to the National Taxpayer Advocate's Annual Report to Congress, the AMT "will, absent a change of law, affect more than 30 million taxpayers by 2010."

So, why are there exponential projected increases in AMT? The regular tax system—including the personal exemptions, standard deduction, and tax rate brackets—is adjusted to account for inflation. The AMT tax rates and threshold exemptions have not been indexed for inflation since the Tax Reform Act of 1986. The AMT exemption amount has been increased slightly, but not enough to allow taxpayers subject to AMT to benefit fully from the reductions in regular income tax rates. As the space between the two tax systems has compressed, it has become correspondingly easier to become a victim of AMT.

The net effect is that over time, more and more taxpayers will have an AMT liability that exceeds their regular tax liability as a result of the absence of inflation indexing. The reality for many taxpayers is that the AMT is unavoidable, and therefore; the key to planning for AMT is to run the numbers carefully and plan for the long term.

Alternative Minimum Tax Computation

Under the AMT system, a taxpayer must determine the alternative minimum taxable income (AMTI) using the separate AMT rules, and then apply the AMT tax rates to the AMTI to determine his or her tentative minimum tax. Generally, if the taxpayer's tentative minimum tax exceeds the taxpayer's regular tax, the excess of the tentative minimum tax over the regular tax becomes the taxpayer's AMT.

The basic formula for calculating AMT is as follows:

- Start with regular taxable income;
- Plus any personal exemption amount claimed;
- Plus any disallowed itemized deductions, including medical and dental (7.5 percent deduction less 10 percent deduction); state and local taxes, certain home equity interest, the bargain element on incentive stock options (ISOs) that you exercise, and miscellaneous itemized deductions;
- Subtract itemized deductions that cannot be claimed on Schedule A because of certain limits for high-income individuals (i.e., the phase-out amount);
- Subtract refunds for state and local taxes;
- Adjust taxable income for specific tax preferences and other adjustment items to arrive at AMTI;
- Subtract the AMT exemption amount (i.e., $40,250 for single or head of household, $58,000 for married filing jointly or qualified widower, $29,000 for married filing separate);
- Multiply the AMTI by the AMT rate (i.e., 26 percent up to $175,000 and 28 percent thereafter);
- Subtract AMT credits;
- Compare the result with the amount of regular tax and pay AMT to the extent it exceeds regular tax.

This formula should only be used to estimate the amount of your AMT liability. To determine your actual liability, you must calculate the liability using a series of IRS forms.

The More the Not-So-Merrier

Taxpayers who are more susceptible to the AMT include those with significant long-term capital gains and dividend income that are subject to preferential low-income tax rates, and/or have tax preference or other adjustment items. AMT taxpayers can be retirees, taxpayers with high state tax deductions (such as New York, California, and DC), corporate executives with large amounts of Incentive Stock Options that are exercised, and business owners with large depreciation deductions or net operating losses, among others. By reducing the regular tax rates, the 2003 Tax Act increased the likelihood that more and more taxpayers will be subject to the AMT.

While the AMT exemption is not adjusted for inflation, the 2003 Tax Act increased the AMT exemption amount as discussed above. When taxable income reaches a certain level, the benefit of this exemption must be reduced or phased out, creating greater likelihood that the AMT will apply to a lot of surprised and unhappy taxpayers.

The 2003 Tax Act did not alter the income levels at which the AMT exemption begins to phase out. For married individuals filing jointly or surviving spouses, the phase-out begins at AMTI of $150,000 and ends at $382,000. For singles or heads of households, the phase-out range is $112,500 to $273,500. For married filing separately, the phase-out range is $75,000 to $191,000.

The phase-out of the AMT exemption amount results in $1.25 of additional AMT for every dollar earned in the phase-out range. In the phase-out range, the marginal AMT rate on ordinary income could be 35 percent, which may be higher than the regular tax rate. Additionally, the marginal AMT rate on capital gains in the phase-out range could be 22 percent, rather than 15 percent. This means that, in some cases, AMT planning for those in the phase-out range can require just the opposite action from those normally subject to AMT. That is, in this phase-out range, effective AMT planning may suggest the deferral of income and acceleration of deductions.

Top-Ten Items That May Cause AMT

An increasing number of individuals are becoming subject to the AMT. As previously mentioned, reasons for the expected swell in the number of AMT taxpayers include the lack of inflation adjustments to rate brackets and exemption amounts, and the disallowance of deductions for state and local taxes. If your calendar year includes any of the items in the following list, you may need tax planning to avoid the AMT:

1. Incentive Stock Options (ISOs), triggering an AMT preference.
2. A transaction that creates significant long-term capital gain income taxed at preferential rates, relative to ordinary income.
3. Investments generating significant qualified dividend income taxed at preferential rates, relative to ordinary income.
4. Location, location, location . . . paying tax to states with high income taxes or property taxes, such as New York, California, and DC.
5. A significant net operating loss (NOL) from a flow-through entity (e.g., family business owner).
6. Expenses that exceed 2 percent of income for investment management or tax-planning services or unreimbursed employee business expenses.
7. Tax-exempt municipal bond income from private activity bonds.
8. Owners of businesses operating as S corporations or partnerships that flow through tax attributes to the owner, including AMT adjustments from the business (e.g., depreciation).
9. Passive activity losses that are allowable for regular tax purposes.
10. Interest on home-equity debt that is deductible for regular income tax purposes, where the loan proceeds were not used to improve the home.

An Unpleasant Surprise for Many

Although the AMT is primarily intended to ensure that wealthy tax-payers pay at least some income tax, it applies to all taxpayers. Year-end may bring an unpleasant surprise to many unsuspecting individuals. As mentioned before, the reduction in marginal tax rates and the lack of inflation adjustments to AMT rates has dramatically increased the number of individuals subject to the AMT. As a result, the time to start planning is now.

If you believe you may be subject to AMT this year, you may want to consider a counterintuitive approach and do the opposite of the normal year-end planning strategy. For example, AMT planning frequently focuses on shifting more income to the tax year in which AMT applies and deferring deductions to the next year. This accelerated income is effectively taxed at the 26 percent or 28 percent AMT rate (rather than the higher regular income tax rates that may apply in a year in which AMT is not anticipated). Deferring deductions until the next year may result in a 35 percent tax benefit in the next year (compared to no tax benefit at all in the current year to the extent AMT applies). However, both of these strategies presume that the AMT will not apply in the succeeding year, which may not be the case. As illustrated next, entirely different tax planning strategies may need to be considered if the AMT is expected to apply in successive years.

In deciding on the right strategy for you, it is essential to compute both your regular tax and AMT liabilities. These calculations serve as the basis to manage income and deductions (to the extent one is able) in order to lessen the AMT bite in a given year.

Because of the vast projected increases in AMT taxpayers for 2005, it is crucial to start income tax planning as soon as possible. Since many AMT tax planning strategies are based on the careful timing of income and deductions, it is important that your plan include multiple year calculations to disclose the full impact of the reversal of timing differences (i.e., accelerating income or deferring deductions). Perform a year-end diagnosis to see if you may fall prey to the AMT and if you believe you may be affected, you should discuss your AMT situation with a professional tax advisor.

AMT Planning Strategies

If you believe you are a target for AMT, what can you do? The following are two lists of the common individual tax planning items to consider, preferably under the guidance of a professional tax advisor, depending on whether you anticipate being subject to AMT in just the 2005 tax year or whether you expect to be subject to AMT in 2005 and beyond.

Taxpayers in AMT in 2005 Only

- Postpone the payment of deductions that yield no tax benefit when a taxpayer is subject to AMT.
- Possibly postpone the payment of deductions that yield some tax benefit when a taxpayer is subject to AMT.
- Consider strategies to accelerate ordinary income and short-term capital gain in 2005.
- Reevaluate the after-tax returns from investments.
- Ask for prepayments of salary and bonus income.
- Consider whether any exercised incentive stock options should be disqualified before year-end to minimize AMT liability if the stock has dropped in value.
- Dispose of investments in private activity bonds.
- Consider intrafamily transactions.

Taxpayers in AMT in 2005 and Beyond

- Recognize capital losses if capital gains are causing the phase out of AMT exemption.
- Pay off home equity loans where the borrowed funds were not used to improve the residence.

- Dispose of investments in private activity bonds.
- Consider making shifts in the investment asset allocation.
- Consider IRA and/or pension distributions.
- Consider intrafamily transactions.

You may also want to take into account the impact of available annual tax elections that may affect the timing of income or deductions. Additional tax planning strategies would apply to taxpayers who fall under the regular tax for 2005, but expect to be in AMT in future years.

These suggested planning items notwithstanding, it is anticipated that AMT will remain a problematic area for family business owners and corporate executives, as well as many other higher income taxpayers. The inadvertent impact of AMT on the larger taxpayer population has yet to be fully appreciated and addressed by Congress. Is an AMT solution forthcoming?

Legislative Alert

There have been many proposals put forth in the past several years to reform the AMT system; however, it appears unlikely that any substantive changes will be made in the near future.

One barrier to successfully addressing the AMT problem is its technical complexity. AMT is difficult to comprehend and may arise due to numerous variables. Politicians are likely to be hesitant to confront the AMT issue because they lack the certainty of a directly correlated political outcome. This may change, however, with the application of AMT to tens of millions of unsuspecting individual taxpayers in the next five years—many of whom may not consider themselves high-income earners and these taxpayers exert political pressure on their elected representatives. Another barrier is that the cost of changing the AMT would be enormous and could potentially produce enormous budget deficits.

Chapter 13 goes beyond the personal strategies discussed in the previous chapters and provides many additional considerations that can generate tax savings for business owners and their companies.

Chapter 13

YEAR-END PLANNING FOR BUSINESS OWNERS

Year-end planning for business owners should incorporate all of the personal strategies previously discussed, but it doesn't end there. There are many additional considerations that can generate tax savings for business owners and for their companies.

Business tax savings of sole proprietorships put more money directly in the hands of the business owner. Where the business is operated as a passthrough entity—an S corporation, partnership, LLC, or LLP—year-end business tax planning must be done at both the entity and the individual levels to enhance potential benefits. That is because these entities don't generally pay income taxes on their earnings. Rather, their income, deductions, and credits are passed through to their owners and reported on their own returns. Individual owners of these types of entities, therefore, need to consider the individual year-end tax planning already outlined in previous chapters and also consider planning designed to benefit the owners' individual tax position and yet complement the company's business goals. It is not an easy task, but it is potentially quite rewarding: For each $1,000 of income that a passthrough business defers or each $1,000 of accelerated deductions, the owner in the top federal income tax bracket will save $350 of current federal income tax. One hundred thousand dollars of combined company year-end income/ deduction shifting reduces current income tax by $35,000 ($1 million reduces it by $350,000). There are potential payroll tax and state and local income tax savings as well. Furthermore, there may be more opportunities for income deferral or deduction acceleration at the business level than at the individual level.

The individual income tax situations of owners of businesses that are operated as C corporations are not as directly affected by the company's year-end tax strategies as are owners of passthrough businesses. But in those cases, taxes saved by the C corporation's successful tax planning result in more capital available for the everyday use of the business, expansion, or dividend payments. The 2003 reductions in the long-term capital gain and dividend tax rates, however, make it imperative for C corporation owners to reevaluate whether to operate as S corporations. In many cases, the current tax regime will make it more attractive to elect to be an S corporation by practically eliminating the prior C corporation federal tax rate advantage on ordinary income. In addition, S corporations provide a substantial tax rate advantage for both long-term capital gains and dividends since they can pass through capital gains and dividends to shareholders undiminished by entity-level taxation. The factors to be considered in making this decision are spelled out in the discussion that follows.

Increased Expensing

The 2003 Tax Act also increased the maximum annual dollar amount that may be expensed—that is, deducted in full rather than having to be depreciated over a number of years—from $25,000 to $100,000 for property placed in service in tax years beginning in 2003. For 2004, and 2005, the limit is increased for inflation ($105,000 in 2005). The previous $200,000 threshold for phase-out of the expensing allowance was increased to $400,000 of expensing-eligible property. The limit is indexed for inflation in 2005 to $420,000.

Off-the-shelf computer software placed in service in a tax year beginning in 2003, 2004, or 2005 now qualifies for expensing. The 2003 Act permits businesses to revoke the expensing election on amended returns without IRS consent. This may enable businesses to retroactively move expensing deductions among tax years for the maximum benefit.

The combination of the expensing allowance and regular depreciation can enable a small business to deduct all or a significant majority of the cost of new property additions in the year of acquisition. For example, if a business acquires new property (with a five-year depreciation life) costing $300,000, it would be entitled to take a combined first-year deduction in 2005 of $144,000. The Section 179 expensing allowance will permit $105,000 to be deducted. The remaining $195,000 of acquisition cost can qualify for a first-year MACRS depreciation deduction of $39,000.

While tax considerations aren't paramount in a business' decision to purchase equipment, they are a factor and are more important this year because of the extra available deduction. The temporary increase in expensing limits of $100,000 ($105,000 for 2005) for qualified depreciable property and computer software, which was scheduled to expire after 2005, has been extended through 2007 under the American Jobs Creation Act of 2004. Additionally, the $400,000 limit, which is $420,000 in 2005, will continue to be indexed for inflation during that same time frame.

Bigger Tax Advantages for Business Automobiles

Deductions for business automobiles are usually quite limited: The first-year deduction generally can't exceed $2,960. But to allow the special depreciation allowance to apply for new business auto purchases, this limit temporarily has been increased to $10,610. To get this break, an automobile must be used more than 50 percent of the time for business. The 2004 Act limited the expensing of a heavy truck or sports utility vehicle (vehicles weighing more than 6,000 pounds) from $100,000 to $25,000 with the balance being depreciated over a five-year recovery period. Accordingly, the business break for sports utility vehicles has been limited in 2005.

Retirement Plans

If this is the year that a business has decided to start a qualified retirement plan, the plan must be formally established by year-end for contributions to be deductible this year. Contributions (up to the limits spelled out in Chapter 3) will be deductible this year if made by the extended tax return due date.

Businesses that miss the year-end deadline can still establish and make deductible contributions to a simplified retirement plan (SEP) by their extended tax return due date. However, SEPs have stricter coverage requirements than regular qualified plans and generally aren't as flexible or customizable. In addition, unlike qualified corporate retirement plans and Keogh plans, SEPs cannot be set up as defined benefit pension plans, so they are less suitable for quickly funding a large benefit for an older owner/employee.

> ### Caution
> Those who plan to set up retirement plans should immediately consult a retirement planning specialist. It takes time to take care of all of the required formalities.

Bonuses and Deferred Compensation

A corporation using the accrual, rather than cash, method of accounting can take a current deduction for bonuses it declares this year, and that are paid within the first 2½ months of the following year. The company gets an accelerated deduction and the employee-recipient gets to defer the income. Note, however, that this planning opportunity isn't available for bonuses paid to majority shareholders or to owners with any interest in an S corporation or a personal service corporation. Compensation that is deferred for more than 2½ months is subject to different rules. In that case, the corporation's deduction is delayed until the compensation is paid to the employee. Year-end also is a good time to consider whether to establish a deferred compensation plan for key employees.

Income Deferral or Acceleration

Generally a C corporation, like an individual, will want to defer income and accelerate deductions, where possible, to reduce current taxes and defer tax liabilities into the following year. For corporations on the accrual method of accounting, this may not be as easy to do as it is for cash method individuals or businesses. However, even for them, certain recurring items may be currently deducted despite the fact that they won't be paid until the following year. There may be times also when a company can come out ahead by reversing the standard strategy and accelerating income into the current year. That's the case, for example, where the corporation is in a lower tax bracket in the earlier year than it expects to be in for the following year.

Although corporate tax rates are graduated, they don't increase in proportion to corporate taxable income. Instead, the first $50,000 is taxed at 15 percent; then the next $25,000 is taxed at 25 percent, and the $25,000 after that is taxed at 34 percent. Corporate taxable income between $100,000 and $335,000 is taxed at 39 percent, to take back the benefit of the 15 percent and the 25 percent tax brackets. Then, between $335,000 and $10 million, the marginal rate drops back to 34 percent. The effect of this is that corporations with taxable income between $335,000 and $10 million are taxed at a flat rate of 34 percent. Then, between $10 million and $15 million, the rate goes up to 35 percent, and then there's another bubble rate of 38 percent between $15 million and $18.33 million to recover the benefit of the 34 percent rate. Corporations with taxable income above $18.33 million are taxed at a flat 35 percent rate.

While all of this seems rather complex, it does present year-end tax saving strategies for corporations in some situations—especially those that are below either the 39 percent or the 38 percent bubbles this year that expect earnings to pick up next year and push them into a higher bracket. If possible, these companies should try to accelerate enough income or defer enough deductions to take advantage of the lower bracket this year.

The 2004 Act provided for a phased-in deduction related to domestic production activity (i.e., manufacturing activity). The tax deduction is 3 percent of the lesser of taxable income or the domestic production activity income in years 2005 and 2006; 6 percent in the years 2007, 2008, and 2009; and 9 percent for years thereafter. This deduction was in lieu of lowering the top corporate tax rate from 35 percent to 32 percent. However, effectively when this deduction is fully phased in for a U.S. manufacturer, the effective rate will be approximately 32 percent.

AMT Planning

Smaller corporations are generally exempt from the AMT if their average annual gross receipts for the prior three-year period is $7.5 million or less. (New corporations are exempt for their first year, but can't average more than $5 million of annual gross receipts for the first three-year period to avoid AMT after that year.) The AMT is a complicated tax that requires many items to be refigured in a way that often reduces the tax benefit from deductions. If a company's average annual gross receipts for the current three-year period are approaching the $7.5 million mark, it should consider the impact of becoming subject to the AMT. If the current year increased gross receipts are an aberration, the company probably would be better off avoiding AMT liability if possible. If the company is growing rapidly and expects to be subject to AMT in the future, it still may benefit the company to hold off for another year before crossing the threshold.

Personal Holding Company Tax

To prevent high-bracket individuals from using closely held C corporations to shelter investment income and avoid the shareholder-level tax on dividend income, these corporations used to be liable for a tax at the top individual rate on their undistributed personal holding company (PHC) income. To be subject to this PHC tax, more than half of a corporation's stock had to be held by five or fewer individuals, and 60 percent of its income must come from items such as rent, royalties, interest, and dividends.

In the past, corporations near the PHC threshold of 60 percent were advised to try to avoid additional PHC income or to increase non-PHC business income to keep the PHC income percentage below 60 percent.

The 2003 Tax Act, however, has reduced the PHC tax rate to 15 percent—the same rate that now applies to dividend income. Corporations potentially subject to the personal holding company tax may consider eliminating the problem while the tax rate on dividends is only 15 percent.

Succession Planning

In addition to income tax planning, year-end is a good time for business owners to contemplate the eventual transfer of their business, whether to family members, other shareholders, key employees, or to an external third party. Owners must also take into account the financial strength of the business, financial position of the buyer, available sources of funding, collateral and financial guarantees, tax consequences to both parties, and cash flow issues. The timing of the transfer and who will retain ownership control are also critical considerations. To manage these complex issues, owners should have access to advisors who can help them make effective and timely decisions. Early planning and a sound grasp of objectives are particularly important in family owned organizations where agreement about family roles contributes to a smooth transition. There are many things to consider.

Buy-Sell Agreements

There are two distinct categories of buy-sell agreements: redemption agreements and cross-purchases. Occasionally, there will be a hybrid of the two types. Under a redemption agreement, the company will fund the buyout using its cash or debt. In a cross-purchase, the shareholder sells stock to other shareholders, not the company. This gives the buying shareholder an increase in the tax basis of his or her stock equal to the purchase price and reduces tax in the future when the stock is subsequently sold. In many cases, there is not enough cash either at the entity level or held by other shareholders to fund the entire purchase. Often, life insurance that is held individually or by a partnership is used to fund the cross-purchase portion of a buyout, with the balance funded by the company through a redemption.

Deferred Compensation

This method refers to income that is deferred until a future point in time. Typically, an employee/shareholder has been under-compensated and a deferred compensation obligation has been established to recognize that fact. Paying a retiring owner deferred compensation is advantageous to the buyer because the deferred compensation payments are tax deductible, whereas payments for his or her stock are not. However, the seller usually will prefer payment for stock, the gains from which are subject only to favorable capital gains tax rates.

Covenant Not to Compete

This is a legal contract that prohibits (for a specific period of time) a seller from competing with the buyer on the business being acquired from the seller. A buyer will frequently offer a portion of the purchase consideration in exchange for the seller signing such a restrictive covenant. This form of consideration is usually deductible to the buyer over a 15-year period but is taxed as ordinary income for the seller.

Earn-Out (Contingent Sale Price)

This element of an acquisition refers to a transaction in which the price paid is not fixed but, instead, fluctuates based on the future performance of the acquired entity. Typically, the actual price will be tied to revenue growth or future profitability over one to five years.

The Importance of Early Planning

Often, people find it difficult to discuss issues relating to illness, retirement, or death. Business owners who avoid addressing these eventualities, however, may make succession planning a low priority, putting family members or other loved ones at financial risk. Lack of time is another often-cited factor; as in estate planning, busy owners can easily put off succession planning to some undefined future time. However, the importance of early planning cannot be overstated since it helps owners meet their stated objectives and facilitate the continuity of their businesses, to the benefit of the owners, employees, customers, and vendors.

From a financial perspective, it is often beneficial to transfer an operation on the brink of value explosion, and some owners attempt to time their transitions accordingly. Although, at this stage the business owner may have no clear picture of future control and management, this should not deter the saving of estate tax. The practical truth is that there will never be a clear picture of future control and management. The effective succession plan has considerable flexibility to deal with changing circumstances and usually involves several different types of trusts to maintain some degree of control. The important thing is not to be delayed by trying to structure the perfect plan up front, but to plan as early in the game as possible.

Don't Wait to Plan!

- Planning in advance promotes reduced estate taxes.
- Planning in advance promotes increased value for the next generation.
- In family perpetuation, owners often have an increased ability to complete long-term transfer time lines.
- Succession plans with longer time lines are inherently more flexible and may have better financial outcomes.
- Conflicting aspirations within a family regarding the timing of the transition may be addressed.

C Corporation versus S Corporation Comparison

With dividends and long-term capital gains now taxed at 15 percent under the 2003 Tax Act, the decision to conduct business as a C corporation or an S corporation should be reevaluated. In many cases, the 2003 Tax Act will make it more attractive to elect to be an S corporation by practically eliminating the prior C corporation federal tax rate advantage on ordinary income. In addition, S corporations now provide a substantial tax rate advantage for both long-term capital gains and dividends since they can pass through capital gains and dividends to shareholders undiminished by entity-level taxation. Ultimately, the conclusion will be dependent on one or more of the following factors:

- The combined federal and state income tax rates that will be applied to income. Movement of the federal tax rates should cause businesses to reevaluate their choice of business entity, and alternative minimum tax and state income taxes need to be factored into the analysis.

- Whether income will be currently distributed. If the business owners desire significant distributions of income, S corporations still have the advantage of avoiding double taxation of the income; however, the 15 percent tax rate on dividends has reduced this advantage.

- Losses from an S corporation can flow through to the shareholders. This remains a significant advantage of S corporations over C corporations for businesses experiencing losses.

- The many shareholder ownership restrictions imposed on S corporations (e.g., shareholder limitations, one class of stock). While S corporations may have tax advantages over C corporations, many businesses are unable to qualify for S corporation status. The 2004 Act increased the maximum number of S corporation shareholders from 75 to 100, and all members of one family (within six generations) can elect to be treated as one shareholder. Serious consideration should be given to restructuring to qualify for S corporation status (i.e., redeem shares, eliminate multiple classes of stock).

- The amount of LIFO recapture upon conversion to S status. With the relatively low inflation rates recently, recapturing the LIFO reserve upon conversion to S status may not be a significant cost at present.

- Whether the business is expected to be sold before the death of the major shareholders. Generally, buyers prefer to buy business assets as opposed to the stock of an ongoing business. By operating as an S corporation, the business owners can sell the business assets and distribute the sale proceeds with only one level of tax. The owners of a C corporation will generally pay two levels (a corporate tax on the asset sale and a shareholder tax—now reduced to 15 percent—on the distributed sale proceeds) of tax.

- Whether the tax on built-in gains is likely to apply. When a C corporation converts to S corporation status, the S corporation is subject to a corporate level tax on any assets sold during its first 10 years as an S corporation. This tax is imposed on the amount of gain that is present in the asset eventually sold as of the first day as an S corporation.

S corporations with C corporation earnings and profits generally will have the ability under the current tax law to purge themselves of the C corporation earnings and profits at a 15 percent tax cost to the shareholders. This may enable the S corporation to avoid the tax on excess passive income and avoid inadvertent termination of the S election from excess passive income in three consecutive tax years. This strategy may be appropriate in 2008, right before the reduced tax rates are set to expire under the sunset provision of the current tax law.

C corporations with large amounts of dividend and long-term capital gain income will have a significant reason to try to convert to S corporation status if possible. The tax rate differential on this income is considerable (35 percent for C corporations versus 15 percent for S corporations).

Chapter 14 moves away from planning suggestions and techniques. It takes a close-up view of the book's basic concepts. Understanding these commonly used words and phrases is critical to making the best use of the tax planning strategies and tools discussed in this book.

A Nuts-and-Bolts Review

Chapter 14

BASIC TAX CONCEPTS

Tax planning is a difficult, time-consuming activity at best. Hopefully, taxpayers who have read this book will have learned a great deal about effective tax planning. This chapter contains definitions of key tax terms. These definitions, which are really a combination of glossary, encyclopedia, and FAQs, constitute an essential reference source for taxpayers.

Earlier chapters described things you may be able to do at the end of the year to reduce your tax bill. At the end of this chapter, you will find valuable suggestions for steps you can take in January as part of your tax minimization program.

Gross Income

Gross income includes all types of taxable income: wages and bonuses, taxable interest, dividends, state tax refunds, alimony, business income, capital gains, traditional IRA distributions, taxable pensions and annuities, rent, partnership and S corporation income, unemployment compensation, and taxable Social Security benefits.

Adjusted Gross Income (AGI)

Adjusted gross income is your gross income less certain "above the line" deductions. These deductions include:

- Deductible IRA contributions (see Chapter 3).
- Health savings account contributions.
- Unreimbursed Employment-related moving expenses (see Chapter 10).
- One-half of self-employment tax.
- 100 percent of health insurance premiums paid by self-employed individuals (see Chapter 10).
- Keogh and SEP contributions for self-employed individuals (see Chapter 3).
- Penalties on early withdrawals of savings.
- Student loan interest.
- Tuition and fees deduction.
- Alimony paid.
- Deduction for buying hybrid vehicles.

Your AGI affects the extent to which you can deduct medical expenses, casualty and theft losses, charitable contributions, and other miscellaneous items. At higher levels of AGI, your ability to benefit from some additional itemized deductions and personal exemptions may be reduced or eliminated (starting in 2006, this phase-out of itemized deductions is reduced).

Modified Adjusted Gross Income

A number of tax breaks are reduced or eliminated as modified adjusted gross income (MAGI) exceeds certain levels. These include the adoption credit, the exclusion for employer-provided adoption assistance, the exclusion for interest on savings bonds used for higher education, IRA deductions, Coverdell ESAs, Roth IRAs, higher education tax credits, the child credit, and the student-loan interest deduction.

MAGI is generally higher than adjusted gross income. That's because various tax breaks that normally reduce AGI are disallowed in calculating MAGI under the different definitions.

A Tax Credit or a Deduction

Tax credits are more valuable than tax deductions because they lower your tax liability dollar for dollar. A $100 tax credit reduces your taxes by a full $100. Examples of tax credits are the HOPE scholarship and lifetime learning tax credits, the child credit, the childcare and dependent care credits, the adoption credit, and the foreign-tax credit.

A tax deduction reduces your taxes by the amount of your deduction multiplied by your marginal tax rate. The lower your tax rate, the smaller your tax benefit from a deduction. In the 35 percent tax bracket, a $100 tax deduction lowers your taxes by $35. In the 15 percent bracket, that same $100 deduction reduces your taxes by only $15.

Observation

It is unwise to pursue tax deductions by spending money on deductible items merely to cut your tax bill. You have to spend more money than you will save in taxes. Keep in mind that a tax deduction is of real value only if it reduces the after-tax cost of an expenditure that you would be inclined to make even if it were not deductible.

Taxable Income

Taxable income is the amount of income on which you actually pay tax. It is calculated by adding your income from all sources and subtracting allowable deductions and exemptions:

Taxable Income Computation

Income

Wages	$350,000
Interest, dividends, and capital gains	26,000
Business income and rental real estate income	5,000
Other income	4,500
Total income	$385,500

Adjustments to Income

Moving expenses	(3,500)
Alimony	(60,000)
Total adjustments to income	$ (63,500)
Adjusted gross income	$322,000
Itemized deductions (after phase-out applied)	(6,200)
Exemption (phased out due to income level)	None
Taxable income	$315,800

Marital Status

Your marital status on the last day of the year determines which of the four tax rate schedules applies. If you are single for most of the year, but marry on December 31, the tax law treats you as married for the entire year.

Changes in marital status can affect year-end planning. Two individuals with substantial incomes who plan to get married in 2006 might benefit from accelerating income into 2005 to avoid the so-called marriage penalty, which has been reduced, but not eliminated (see pages 256–257).

Widows and widowers are allowed to file a joint return with their deceased spouse in the year of the spouse's death, and to use joint return rates for up to two additional years if they have a qualifying dependent. Widows or widowers who may be eligible to use the

Table 14.1	*2005 Tax Rates and 2006 Tax Rates*					
Taxable Income ($)	2005 Tax ($)	Marginal Tax (%)	Taxable Income ($)	2006 Tax ($)	Marginal Tax (%)	Effective Tax Rate (%)
Single Individuals						
0	0	10	0	0	10	0
7,300	730	15	7,550	755	15	10.0
29,700	4,090	25	30,650	4,220	25	13.8
71,950	14,653	28	74,200	15,108	28	20.4
150,150	36,549	33	154,800	37,676	33	24.3
Over 326,450	94,728	35	Over 336,550	97,653	35	29.0
Married Filing Jointly						
0	0	10	0	0	10	0
14,600	1,460	15	15,100	1,510	15	10.0
59,400	8,180	25	61,300	8,440	25	13.8
119,950	23,318	28	123,700	24,040	28	19.4
182,800	40,916	33	188,450	42,170	33	22.4
Over 326,450	88,320	35	Over 336,550	91,043	35	27.1

more favorable married filing jointly rates in 2005, but not in 2006, could benefit from accelerating income into the earlier year (see Table 14.1).

Marginal and Effective Tax Rates

Marginal tax is the tax imposed on the next dollar of income. Effective tax rate is the average tax rate on all of your income. For example, assume that you are married, filing a joint return, and receive:

Taxable Income	$300,000
Bonus	$ 50,000
Total Taxable Income	$350,000

The bonus is taxed at 35 percent. You would pay $17,500 ($50,000 × 35 percent) in taxes on that bonus. Your marginal tax rate is 35 percent.

Your marginal tax rate also determines the tax benefit of a deductible expense. For example, if you were in the 28 percent bracket and had $5,000 of medical expenses in excess of 7.5 percent of your AGI, which you claimed as an itemized deduction, you would reduce your taxable income by $5,000, saving $1,400 in tax dollars ($5,000 × 28 percent).

> ### Caution
> Your marginal tax rate might not determine the tax benefit of a deductible expense if your income is above $145,950 for 2005, since at that income level you begin losing some of the benefit of your itemized deductions.

Your effective tax rate is the average rate at which all of your income is taxed. To determine this rate, divide your tax liability by your taxable income. If your 2005 taxable income on a joint return is $150,000 and the amount of tax due is $31,731.50, your marginal tax rate is 28 percent, but your effective tax rate is only 21.15 percent ($31,731.50/$150,000 = 0.2115).

Your marginal tax rate can be higher than the 35 percent statutory rate due to the itemized deduction and personal exemption phase out (see page 14). The following charts show 2005 and 2006 deductions and exemptions:

2005 ITEMIZED DEDUCTION AND PERSONAL EXEMPTIONS

	Single	Married Joint	Separate	Head of Household
Standard Deductions				
Regular standard deduction	$5,000	$10,000	$5,000	$7,300
Additional standard deduction (elderly and/or blind taxpayers)	$1,250	$1,000	$1,000	$1,250
Kiddie tax deduction	$800	$800	$800	$800
Itemized Deduction Phase-Out				
Deductions reduced for AGI exceeding	$145,950	$145,950	$72,975	$145,950
Personal Exemption				
Each person	$3,200	$3,200	$3,200	$3,200
Personal Exemption Phase-Out				
Exemptions reduced for AGI exceeding	$145,950	$218,950	$109,475	$182,450

2006 ITEMIZED DEDUCTION AND PERSONAL EXEMPTIONS

	Single	Married Joint	Separate	Head of Household
Standard Deductions				
Regular standard deduction				
	$5,150	$10,300	$5,150	$7,550
Additional standard deduction (elderly and/or blind taxpayers)				
	$1,250	$1,000	$1,000	$1,250
Kiddie tax deduction				
	$850	$850	$850	$850
Itemized Deduction Phase-Out				
Deductions reduced for AGI exceeding				
	$150,500	$150,500	$75,250	$150,500
Personal Exemption				
Each person				
	$3,300	$3,300	$3,300	$3,300
Personal Exemption Phase-Out				
Exemptions reduced for AGI exceeding				
	$150,500	$225,750	$112,875	$188,150

The existing rules reducing itemized deductions allow you to claim at least 20 percent of your itemized deductions regardless of your income level. This limit does not affect itemized deductions for medical expenses, casualty losses, and investment interest.

Observation

The limit on itemized deductions increases the top marginal tax rate for high-income individuals by 1.05 percent. The phase-out of personal exemptions increases the top marginal tax rate for these families and individuals by approximately 0.75 percent for income in the phase-out range for each exemption claimed.

Observation

The 2001 Tax Act will start to eliminate the phase-outs of itemized deductions and personal exemptions beginning in 2006.

Social Security Taxes

If you are employed, you are subject to a 7.65 percent tax rate (6.2 percent for Social Security and 1.45 percent for Medicare). Your employer also pays the same rates to the government. If you are self-employed, you pay a 15.3 percent self-employment tax (12.4 percent for Social Security and 2.9 percent for Medicare). Self-employed individuals are entitled to deduct one-half of their self-employment tax as an "above the line" deduction. The maximum annual earnings subject to the Social Security tax is $90,000 in 2005. This amount will increase to $94,200 for 2006. All earnings are subject to the Medicare portion of the tax.

If you work while collecting Social Security benefits and are between age 62 and your full retirement age (e.g., 65 years and 4 months for those born in 1939), your benefits are reduced by $1 for every $2 that you earn above $12,480 in 2006 ($1,040 per month). This limit will increase annually. In the year you reach your full retirement age, you lose $1 for every $3 of earnings above $33,240

($2,770 per month) in 2006, but only for months before your full retirement age. Once you have attained your full retirement age, earnings do not cause a reduction in your benefits.

If you work while collecting benefits, you also should consider that your earnings will be subject to income tax and payroll taxes, and these earnings also may subject some of your Social Security benefits to income tax. If your AGI, plus half of your Social Security benefits, plus your tax-exempt interest equals more than $25,000 if you're single, or $32,000 if married, half of the excess amount up to 50 percent of your Social Security benefits are taxable. If your specially figured income exceeds $34,000 if single, or $44,000 if married, up to 85 percent of your Social Security benefits may be subject to income tax.

Marriage Penalty

The marriage penalty results because the marginal tax rate is higher for married couples than it is for two single individuals with the same total income. Let's see how a married couple fared under the old rules: Assume that two single persons, each with taxable income of $100,000 in 2002, were each taxed at the 30 percent marginal rate. If these two people were married, $28,050 of their total taxable income in 2002 (the amount above $171,950) would have been taxed at the 35 percent rate. Total tax for the two singles: $48,630. As a married couple, the tax would jump to $51,813, resulting in a penalty of $3,183.

If, however, one spouse has a much higher income than the other, there may be a marriage bonus. For example, a single person with $200,000 of taxable income in 2002 paid tax at a 35 percent marginal tax rate on $58,750 of it. If the same person was married and his or her spouse had no income, the couple would have been subject to a marginal tax rate of 35 percent on only $28,050 of the income using joint-return rates.

The marriage penalty has been eased somewhat by increasing the size of the 15 percent tax bracket for married taxpayers to double that of singles, and by increasing the size of the standard deduction for married taxpayers to double that of singles (see page 253 for details). Despite this, the marriage penalty still can be quite substantial for couples in the higher tax brackets.

Viewing the same couple's taxes today, let's see how the marriage penalty has declined. If they were single, together they would owe a tax of $45,013. As a married couple, the tax would jump to $46,592, resulting in a marriage penalty of $1,579.

Some married couples may benefit by filing separately. For example, it may make sense to file separately if one spouse is in a lower tax bracket and has large medical bills. The AGI threshold limiting the deduction of these medical expenses would be lower, allowing a larger deduction.

Observation

It is important to work out the numbers before deciding what to do. Over the years, Congress has added "penalty" provisions to the Tax Code to discourage married people from filing separate returns. So filing separately may seem like a good idea for one reason or another but might result in higher taxes overall than if you file jointly.

Accountable Plan

Business expenses reimbursed by your employer may be included as income on your Form W-2 unless your employer reimburses under an accountable plan. An accountable plan requires documentation before a return is filed of all advanced or reimbursed expenses and the return of any excess amounts. Expenses reimbursed under a nonaccountable plan can be included in your income and are deductible, as are unreimbursed employee business expenses, in the miscellaneous itemized deductions category, if you have receipts and other required substantiation.

Observation

A nonaccountable plan is not as good as it may at first sound because miscellaneous itemized deductions can be claimed only to the extent that they total more than 2 percent of your AGI. So if your AGI is $100,000, your first $2,000 of miscellaneous expenses are not deductible. In addition, you would receive no tax benefits from the deduction of miscellaneous business expenses if you are subject to the alternative minimum tax (AMT). The AMT is described in detail in Chapter 12.

Tax Effects of Alimony

Alimony is included in the gross income of the person receiving it and is deductible by the person paying it.

Observation

Alimony is deducted "above the line" in arriving at AGI. Therefore, it can be claimed whether you itemize your deductions or take the standard deduction.

Payments to an ex-spouse are not treated as alimony for tax purposes if the spouses are still in the same household. It is also important to note that large decreases in the amount of alimony in the second and third years following a divorce trigger IRS concern that property settlement amounts, which are nondeductible, are being treated as alimony. There are guidelines on what payments under a divorce or separation agreement qualify as alimony for tax purposes.

For example, making rent or mortgage payments for a spouse or ex-spouse may be deductible alimony, but the value of rent-free accommodations (e.g., allowing a spouse or former spouse to live without paying rent in a house you own) is not deductible.

Social Security Taxes for Domestic Employees

You must pay and withhold Social Security tax for domestic employees earning more than $1,400 during 2005. This figure will be increased for future inflation. You may report this tax liability each year as a balance due on your Form 1040, Schedule H. Be sure to increase your wage withholding or make quarterly estimated tax payments to pay the tax associated with these employees and avoid an estimated tax underpayment penalty.

Estimated Tax Payments

The government requires estimated tax payments because it prefers receiving tax payments throughout the year. Individuals with a $1,000 or greater balance due on their tax returns may be subject to an estimated tax underpayment penalty, unless certain standards are met. An interest-based underpayment of estimated tax penalty is charged if no exception applies.

In general, there are three methods that can be used to avoid an underpayment penalty:

1. Estimated tax payments and/or withholding are equal to at least 100 percent of last year's total tax liability. However, if your AGI for the preceding year exceeded $150,000, your current year's estimated taxes must be 110 percent of your preceding year's total tax liability to fall within this safe harbor.

2. 90 percent of your current-year total tax liability is paid through estimated tax payments and/or withholding.

3. 90 percent of annualized income (determined each quarter based on actual income) is paid through estimated tax payments and/or withholding. These methods are applied to each

quarter using one-fourth of the amounts described previously. A different method can be applied each quarter.

Observation

The annualization method is generally best if a large part of your income is received in the latter part of the year.

Dates on Which You Must Pay Your Estimated Taxes

April 15:	Based on actual income through March 31.
June 15:	Based on actual income through May 31.
September 15:	Based on actual income through August 31.
January 15:	Based on actual income through December 31.

Caution

If you use the "90 percent of current year's tax liability" method to calculate your estimated tax payments and recognize a large gain at year-end, you could be saddled with estimated tax penalties from a shortfall in earlier quarter payments. If you have a choice as to when you recognize the gain, remember to consider estimated tax payment obligations.

Observation

If you fall behind in estimated tax installments at the beginning of a year, you may avoid or reduce an estimated tax penalty by having additional tax withheld from your wages during the latter part of the year. Wage withholding is treated as occurring evenly over the course of the year, so one-quarter of each dollar withheld is treated as having been withheld in each quarter of the year.

You can make additional payments at any time during the year to reduce or, in some cases, eliminate potential estimated tax underpayments.

Be careful not to overpay, though, because the excess payment is essentially an interest-free loan to the government.

> ### *Observation*
> You may be able to "cure" an estimated tax underpayment by rolling over one IRA to another IRA account (within 60 days) and electing to have tax withheld that will be treated as paid ratably during the year even if the rollover was late in the year.

> ### *Observation*
> Use of either the annualization method or the 90 percent of current year's tax liability method is a good idea if your year-over-year income decreases or increases from one year to the next by only a small amount. But if you have a sizable increase in income (for instance, if 100 percent [or 110 percent for those with an AGI over $150,000] of your prior year's tax will be less than 90 percent of the tax due on your current year's income), using the "percentage of the prior year's tax liability" method allows the payment of lower estimated tax. This method is also far simpler because you are making payments based on a known amount, not estimates.

January Tax Strategy Idea Checklist

Most tax help books present year-end planning ideas. We have decided to go one step further and suggest strategies that make sense to implement as early in the year as possible. Early adoption of the ideas presented in the list that follows may make sense to maximize your opportunities to defer tax, generate income that is tax-free, and/or shift assets or income out of your estate:

☑ Contribute to an IRA (see page 67).

☑ Contribute to a Coverdell Education Savings Account (see page 112).

☑ Contribute to a Section 529 plan to the amount of the state tax deduction (if available, see page 106).

☑ Make a contribution to your Keogh (see page 65–66).

☑ Consider a Roth IRA conversion (see page 115).

☑ Think about making additional gifts if you have not fully used your unified credit equivalent of $1 million (see page 141).

☑ Make payments that were due in 2005 that you deferred to 2006 because of the AMT (see page 229).

☑ Purchase the annual maximum of Series I bonds (see page 215).

☑ Make $12,000 ($24,000 for married couples) annual exclusion gifts (see page 134).

☑ Exercise Incentive Stock Options, so that you have a full year to decide whether to sell the stock and be taxed as a nonqualified stock option (see page 49).

Conclusion

Some people enjoy tax planning, and other people would prefer to do almost anything else. What most of us consider a burden needn't be a nightmare or a mystery. People can understand their tax options and intelligently choose those options best suited to their needs. This book is intended to be a liberating guide, grounded in our belief that every tax problem has a solution, if accurate and accessible information is available.

We have given you much to think about. Chapter 1 lays out the tax changes that have taken place in 2005. The rest of the book provides a wide range of information and strategies and covers diverse areas, such as investments, retirement planning, home ownership, education savings, estate planning, and year-end tax planning. It also explains many basic tax concepts. The tax laws are incredibly complex. The Internal Revenue Code, along with its regulations and related cases, procedures, and rulings, can fill whole library rooms. As difficult as the law is, specific financial, family, and business situations can complicate things further, making tax planning a highly personal and individualized undertaking.

This book offers you a foundation—information and strategies that will make most individuals aware of ideas that may work for them and help them avoid costly tax mistakes. You should supplement this new foundation in taxes by considering how your personal situation plays into tax decisions. Tax planning never occurs in a vacuum, but is just a part, albeit an important part, of an overall financial planning process.

The tax strategies described in this book have been developed from the combined experience of many PricewaterhouseCoopers professionals. However, because every individual has unique circumstances, it could be important for you to consult a tax professional before implementing some tax strategies described in this book or elsewhere.

ABOUT THE AUTHORS

Michael B. Kennedy is a Personal Financial Services Partner in PricewaterhouseCoopers Private Company Services Practice which provides comprehensive financial planning services to high net worth individuals, corporate executives, business owners, and entrepreneurs. Michael has been with the firm for more than 30 years. Michael is a CPA and member of the American, Pennsylvania, and New Jersey Institutes of Certified Public Accountants and holds the Personal Financial Specialist designation. He has both a BS in Economics and an MBA from Rider University. Michael is an adjunct member of the Villanova University Graduate Tax Program. He is a member of the board of trustees of Rider University and was most recently honored by his alma mater with a lifetime achievement award from the School of Business.

Bernard S. Kent is a Personal Financial Services Partner in PricewaterhouseCoopers Private Company Services Practice. He has over 30 years of experience encompassing all phases of tax planning and personal financial counseling. Bernie has been frequently quoted in numerous national periodicals including the *Wall Street Journal,* the *New York Times, Investor's Business Daily, Forbes, Fortune, U.S.*

News and World Report, Barron's, Business Week, Kiplinger's, and *Inc.* In October 2005, he was chosen by *Worth* magazine as one of the 100 top wealth advisors in the country. It is the fourth time he has been selected. He is the past chairman of the Personal Financial Planning Committee of the Michigan Association of Certified Public Accountants. He received his BA in Economics from Oakland University and JD from the University of Michigan Law School.

Karl T. Weger is a Personal Financial Services Partner in PricewaterhouseCoopers Private Company Services Practice. He has over 20 years of experience working with businesses and business owners to address wealth planning issues. Karl focuses his efforts on helping individuals grow and protect their wealth from the many things that can diminish personal wealth (i.e., poor investments, income taxes, wealth transfer taxes, divorce, creditor claims, casualties, and spendthrift heirs). He is admitted to the Pennsylvania Bar and is a member of the American Institute of Certified Public Accountants. Karl holds a BS in Accounting from Villanova University and a JD from the Villanova University School of Law.

INDEX

G

H